Haunted
Oregon

Ghosts and Strange Phenomena of the Beaver State

Andy Weeks

Illustrations by Marc Radle

STACKPOLE BOOKS

For Heidi—
My beautiful muse; my dream fulfilled

Published by
STACKPOLE BOOKS
5067 Ritter Road
Mechanicsburg, PA 17055
www.stackpolebooks.com

Printed in the United States of America

10 9 8 7 6 5 4 3 2 1

FIRST EDITION

Cover design by Tessa Sweigert

Library of Congress Cataloging-in-Publication Data

Weeks, Andy.
  Haunted Oregon : ghosts and strange phenomena of the Beaver State / Andy Weeks ; illustrations by Marc Radle. — First edition.
    pages cm
  Includes bibliographical references.
  ISBN 978-0-8117-1263-7
  1. Haunted places—Oregon. 2. Ghosts—Oregon. I. Title.
  BF1472.U6W4357 2014
  133.109795—dc23
                        2014004969

Contents

Introduction

THERE OFTEN IS NO BLACK AND WHITE WHEN IT COMES TO THE PARANOR-mal. Mostly it exists in a gray area where strange things occur but cannot quite be explained. While some people adamantly refuse to believe in ghosts, others will swear on a stack of holy books that they've come face-to-face with a spirit entity or, at the very least, the manifestations of one—phantom voices or footsteps, objects that move of their own volition, and the like.

It's okay not to believe in the paranormal, of course, but it strikes me as funny when I hear the skeptics. Many of them claim to be people of faith. They seem readily able to believe in the super-natural stories of their holy books, yet find it difficult to believe that anything similar can happen today, saying that such things as ghosts or demons don't exist. Even the Bible, which is full of mira-cles and marvelous good, contains stories of curses, demons, ghosts, and witches. The truth as I see it, however, is that if there is good in the world, there also must be evil. If there is a God, a devil also exists. If there are angels, there must be demons. If there is life after death, there must be spirits. And if we are eternal beings, then such things as gods, ghosts, and demons must exist in both time and eternity. I do believe in a loving God but I won't say that the supernatural, originating from both good and evil sources, does not happen today. I believe it does, in many fashions, and not all of it can be summed up in a neat and tidy little book. Not everyone has a true ghost story to tell, but just because you haven't had one—or several—doesn't mean that ghosts aren't real. It just might be that our perceptions of what a ghost is are skewed.

This book, my third with Stackpole Books, contains some stories that are lighthearted, but also some that are deeply serious. All of them are allegedly true, taken from the historical record and stories recounted. You don't have to be a believer to read these stories, though it's worth noting that a national public survey claims the number of people who believe in some kind of paranormal activity is on the rise. Three in every four people believe in the paranormal, according to a June 16, 2005, Gallup poll. Out of 1,002 adults surveyed in the United States, 37 percent of responders said they believe houses can be haunted. In addition, 32 percent said they believe a dead person could come back from the Great Beyond in certain places and situations. The poll also found that 31 percent believe in telepathy, 26 percent believe in clairvoyance, 21 percent believe that people can communicate mentally with someone who has died, and 21 percent believe in witches. Extrasensory perception (ESP) received the most supporters at 41 percent.

In November of the same year, Gallup published a follow-up piece with additional information about its previous findings. "Women [42 percent] are more likely than men [31 percent] to believe in haunted houses, communicating with the dead, and astrology," the poll reads. "Men, on the other hand, show a slightly greater proclivity than women to believe in extraterrestrial beings." There's also a significant part of the younger crowd who say they are believers in the paranormal. The National Study of Youth and Religion surveyed more than three thousand teenagers (ages thirteen to seventeen) and found that many "say they are open to believing in astrology, psychics and communicating with the dead."

Types of Hauntings

It is commonly agreed in paranormal circles that, although not all hauntings fit into a niche, there are at least six common types:

• **Residual:** Often when a traumatic event occurs, the negative energy of the act is "blasted" into the atmosphere, which then, like a recording, plays itself over and over again. I believe, however, that residual activity can also stem from the positive energy of life itself. Residual activity is one of the more common and harmless types of hauntings.

- **Intelligent:** Whenever ghost hunters investigate a site, they ask questions in the hope that unseen presences will answer them in some way, whether by means of a disembodied voice, knocking sounds, or moving an object. This interactive play is an example of an intelligent haunting because the entity is trying to communicate in real time with the living.

- **Poltergeist:** If you see objects move of their own volition, this is most likely caused by a poltergeist, believed to be projected by the human mind. It has been theorized that poltergeists are associated with adolescents, especially young women who experience significant stress. Stephen King played up this theory in his first novel, *Carrie*, which described a young woman with the power of telekinesis, a phenomenon similar to poltergeist activity in which a person has the ability to move objects with the mind. Poltergeists often are associated with mischief and sometimes more violent behavior. They like to harass their victims by making loud noises, moving furniture or other items, and throwing objects at people. Many of those who suspect poltergeist activity in their homes set up video cameras to capture the paranormal activity when no one else is home. Take a look at some of the videos of alleged poltergeist activity on YouTube. Some might be the work of clever special effects, but not all of them.

- **Demon:** Ask paranormal investigators about the most frightening entity they could encounter, and they'll more than likely tell you it would be a demon—a malicious spirit that scares, torments, and often manipulates people to commit sinful acts. A demon can appear as black fog or mist, a shadow, or a misleading spirit. Its sole purpose is to inflict fear and pain. It takes a religious act, such as a cleansing or blessing, to rid a place of these evil spirits.

- **Shadow People:** It is still unclear what exactly shadow people are, but they appear as shapeless, dark masses and are often seen only with peripheral vision. They can move between walls but have no human features. Clairvoyants consider them nonhuman entities. Christopher Balzano, author of *Ghostly Adventures*, describes them as "Not quite demons, or at least not classified as traditional demons, they might get their strength from the sadness or fear of the living, or from the energy of other spirits. They never want to communicate, only to be there." Marie Cuff, executive director of the International Paranormal Reporting Group, a TAPS member, said she has not "bought into the assumption that it must be evil just because it is a shadow person." Instead, she said she believes shadow people are apparitions, spirits, or ghosts showing themselves "in a different light."

• **Doppelganger:** Ever been haunted by a mirror? A doppelganger is your evil twin, considered to be the harbinger of misfortune or death. These hauntings, while frightening, are extremely rare. It is the one haunting not discussed further in this book because I found no accounts of doppelganger encounters in Oregon.

One thing we should not do, according to some folks who've studied the paranormal, is seek after the dead. If you're considering ghost hunting, you might want to think again. While it is interesting and even fun to read about ghosts and strange phenomena, it is quite another to actually experience the paranormal. In some instances, those who seek after ghosts may get more than they bargained for, and it is recommended to keep the study of ghosts at book's length. Séances, Ouija boards, and even amateur ghost hunting—as well as other efforts to contact the dead—have often welcomed uninvited guests and, in some instances, harm has befallen the unsuspecting person or persons. Much like a chemistry experiment, unless you're an expert you don't know exactly what will happen when mixing different elements together. And even if you are an expert, accidents can still happen.

"Opening a door is never a good idea, as there is no telling who or what will walk through it," reads a post on the PinellasPasco-Paranormal website, run by specialists who study the phenomena of hostile hauntings. "Many an amateur ghost hunter have brought problems upon themselves, by seeking out spirits at cemeteries and supposed haunted locations. Some spirits will follow you home to play the game some more, and others resent the intrusion and will follow to retaliate."

Ghost hunting has at times been dangerous, proving physically and mentally disturbing for the participants. In some instances it has been disastrous, with investigators becoming the investigated when spirits attached themselves to the ghost hunters, following them home to make them become the haunted. The PinellasPasco-Paranormal website shares an EVP in which the entities of several spirits attached themselves to an amateur ghost hunter and followed the investigator home because, as one spirit said, "That's why we came in here, you said it was alright."

In essence, ghost hunting in the real world is nothing like it is on television, and those who consider seeking after the unknown have to accept the responsibility that the hostile side of the paranormal is exactly what they may find.

Oregon History in Brief

There are several eras of U.S. history that involve Oregon. The westward journey of emigrants began in the late 1830s with a single missionary couple, and thousands later followed in their footsteps. On foot and by handcart and wagon, these emigrants traveled America's 2,100-plus-mile Overland Route—better known as the Oregon Trail—from Missouri to the Pacific Northwest. Though we don't know for sure, it is estimated that by the 1860s, when the trail's use began to cease, nearly 100,000 people had used the route in their efforts to achieve their goal of a better life in the West. Most went to Oregon, but others, after traveling so far on the main stem, broke away to head in different directions. Some went to California to find gold, and others, such as the Mormons, went to Utah's Salt Lake Valley to find refuge and freedom of religion. No matter who used it, the Oregon Trail served their needs. Portions of the trail are still visible today in many parts of the country, though sadly, time and Mother Nature are decreasing the trail's imprint.

Before the Oregon Trail, Meriwether Lewis and William Clark had been commissioned by President Thomas Jefferson to make the United States' first overland expedition to the Pacific Northwest. They made their now-famous journey, the Corps of Discovery Expedition, between 1804 and 1806. They bedded for the winter in 1805–06 at Fort Clatsop near the mouth of the Columbia River in present-day Astoria. Their journey was soon followed by David Thompson of Great Britain, who explored the Columbia River from 1807 to 1811, noting with satisfaction the area's abundance of fur-bearing animals. Others came after that, and following the Anglo-American Treaty of 1818 the region was occupied jointly by the United States and Great Britain. Americans called it Oregon Country, while the British named it the Hudson's Bay Company's

Columbia District, administered from Fort Vancouver near what is now Vancouver, Washington. The joint occupation ended with the signing of the Oregon Treaty in 1846, when Britain ceded all claims to lands south of the forty-ninth parallel.

The name Oregon, according to colonial major Robert Rogers, comes from the Native Indians who lived in the area, but this is not definitive, as there are other speculations as to the origin of the name. In a 1765 petition by Rogers to Great Britain, he wrote: "The Rout [sic] . . . is from the Great Lakes towards the Head of the Mississippi, and from thence to the River called by the Indians Ouragon [later the Columbia River]. . . ." By 1778 the region, which awaited others to arrive and settle it, was known as Oregon.

In many respects, Oregon, with its long and active history, seems like the perfect place for ghosts. But there's also other strangeness that happens here—a host of nature's unsolved mysteries including Bigfoot, lake monsters and other hybrid creatures, and a plethora of unexplained sightings of out-of-this-world phenomena best described as unidentified flying objects (UFOs). You'll read about all of these types of paranormal experiences in this book, plus a few others that don't fit into a specific category.

Whether you are a believer in the paranormal or a born-again skeptic, you've picked up this book for a reason. What is it? Frankly, it doesn't matter to me as long as you enjoy what you read here, for the job of any writer is to educate and entertain his or her audience. I hope that through these pages you are educated and entertained about the paranormal as well as Oregon's fascinating history. Maybe you'll share these stories with others, perhaps by a campfire, on All Hallows Eve, or when the wind blows at night. That noise you hear in the other room? It is just the wind, after all.

Or is it?

Portland

EVERY CITY WORTH ITS SALT HAS A FASCINATING HISTORY AND MANY STO-
ries of ghosts, haunted places, and instances of strange phenomena. Perhaps the most haunted city in the Beaver State is Portland.
It is an iconic city, dotted with old buildings, dark tunnels, and people who are artistic, vibrant, and, like the city itself, interesting.

Much has been written about Portland on websites, in travel
articles, and in books. Endless, it seems, is the history of this city
along the Willamette River. At one time the *Oregonian*, the state's
largest and best-known newspaper, called Portland a dirty city, but
today it is known as the "City of Roses," a name that is both imaginative and literal. Roses bloom here all year long, able to extend
their colors because of the area's moderate climate, and Portland is
home to the International Rose Test Garden. During the dot-com
boom of the 1990s, many entrepreneurs were attracted to Portland
because of its highbrow, artistic atmosphere, one that allows for the
freethinking of its citizens. Even after the dot-com boom ended,
many of the people remained. That in itself must say something of
the area and why it's worth making it your home.

As far as this book is concerned, however, it's the city's ghosts
that we are most interested in—the spirits that date back to the
area's earliest days, and some from more recent times. What is it
about Portland that has made spirits want to stay? I don't know

that we'll come to a definitive answer, but the topic of Portland haunts is worth exploring anyway. I hope you have fun meeting the ghosts inhabiting cemeteries, old schoolhouses and hotels, local businesses and thoroughfares, and even underground tunnels. These are just some of the things that make Portland one of Oregon's most intriguing and haunted places.

Portland's Shady Underground

When you think of the underground, what probably comes to mind is something sinister or shady, or something criminal in nature— perhaps a drug cartel or a mafia's secretive business. You wouldn't be too far off. There is perhaps no place in Portland as shady as the city's underground tunnels, more infamously known as the Shanghai Tunnels.

In essence, "to shanghai" is to kidnap. The verb, as Merriam-Webster defines it, means "to put aboard a ship by force, often with the help of liquor or a drug," "to put by force or threat of force into or as if into a place of detention," or "to put by trickery into an undesirable position." The term stems from about 1871, when the method was used in China to secure sailors for voyages to eastern Asia. The method also was used in early Portland history, according to some stories.

Researching the history of the Shanghai Tunnels becomes a little frustrating because many different versions exist to explain why the tunnels were made. Some say they were created for flood control, while others say they were built for cargo unloading or streetcar lines. One popular story is that business owners would use them to funnel merchandise from ships docked on the Willamette River to their places of business to avoid the commotion of the streetcars and trains above ground. According to lore, the tunnels were also used to hide and transfer kidnapped victims to the ships, where they'd be sold or traded. Prostitutes also used the underground.

"Lurid stories of kidnappers seizing drunken or drugged men and whisking them through a network of underground tunnels are a cornerstone of old Portland lore," reads an October 4, 2007, article in the *Oregonian*. "The kidnappers, as legend has it, sold hapless men to ship captains desperate for crewmen in the late 19th and early 20th centuries."

Travel writers and television shows have immortalized the legend of the Shanghai Tunnels, but some question whether the tunnels even exist. According to one historian, as quoted in the same article, he has been searching for evidence of the tunnels for years. "Normally, they would expect to find legal or municipal records referring to the digging that would have been necessary between buildings," the article reads. "They'd also expect to find mentions, for example, in a 1912 vice commission report on Old Town, other crime reports or in stories about shanghaiing at the time." None of this has been uncovered. The skeptics say that even if the tunnels did exist, it doesn't mean they were used for shanghaiing.

Still, there is a group that offers tours of the tunnels—though visitors do not traverse the dark abyss but instead get a history lesson on the area and are shown some basements in downtown businesses that supposedly lead off into the tunnels. There are such things as connected basements, others say, but are there enough of them to form a network of tunnels?

The stories persist, however, that such underground passages actually do exist. And in their darkness roam darker shades. Some of these ghosts are said to venture upward to haunt the businesses that sit above the tunnels. Accounts of business owners or staff members who have encountered apparitions or had experiences with the paranormal are abundant in downtown Portland, and most of the stories seem to have ties to the underground phantoms.

Among the more common stories are tales of the shades of ghostly prostitutes that appear in some establishments and sometimes try to lead men into the basement depths. In other buildings, people report seeing the spirits of men in period clothes. People claim to have been grabbed by unseen hands, and objects move of their own volition or are found out of place when clearly no one else was around to disturb them.

During the spring Portland Rose Festival, if you see sailors dressed in old-style uniforms, they might be from the spirit world, risen from the tunnels to join their living compatriots in the celebrations. Evee Vann, a native Portlander, said she has heard such stories for years and even knows of people who claim to have seen such ghostly apparitions among the throng of the living sailor celebrants.

"There are stories that sailors were knocked out and died in the tunnels," she said. "It is said their spirits come out of the tunnels to drink with the living sailors."

The Floating Phantom

Mike Eadie, owner of Hoodoo Antiques & Design in Portland, said it took a knock on the head—literally—to get him to consider the possibility of paranormal activity.

A few years ago, on a quiet Sunday, while a family browsed the collection of antiques at his downtown shop, a large pole in the shop suddenly fell, hitting Eadie on the head. There was no reason for that to happen, he said in a phone interview. "The family in the store came over to see if I was okay," he said. "I was more startled than anything else. I'm going to chalk it up to something odd. There certainly [weren't] any big trucks or machinery in the area to cause a vibration that'd cut things loose. I'm usually not very sensitive to that kind of stuff [paranormal activity], so that's why I say it took something to hit me over the head."

A possible reason for the wakeup call, he said, was to bring attention to a ghostly woman that apparently felt forgotten. When Eadie told his story, it quickly spread and people began to visit his shop, inquiring about the paranormal activity. Was there something about the antiques that attracted spirits from the past?

One night, two men walking past Eadie's shop saw something move in the window. They came closer and peered inside, not expecting to see what they did. The figure of a woman was floating across the store about nine feet above the ground. The story spread like wildfire and soon even more people were coming to Eadie's shop. Paranormal tours in the area would stop by to ask him about the smack on the head and the ghost woman, who Eadie believes lived during Portland's earliest days.

Eadie first opened his shop in 1994, and moved into his current location at 122 NW Couch Street in 2000. His mother-in-law, however, had opened a shop at Portland's Saturday Market as part of a revitalization effort because many of the old businesses had been shuttered during Prohibition. The building his mother-in-law operated held a secret she uncovered in an upstairs room: an old photograph of a woman dressed in period clothing. For some reason, she brought the portrait to Eadie's shop one day, saying she felt it needed to be there. She allegedly was right. The men who claimed to see the floating woman described her as dressed in period clothing and wearing a bonnet on her head. Eadie showed them the photograph of the woman. It was the very same one they saw elevated in his shop. Her hair, Eadie told me, was styled in such a way as to look like she was wearing a bonnet.

Do any other antiques in his shop also have strangeness associated with them, perhaps a ghost that has attached itself to an object? "I really don't know," Eadie said. "I never thought of that, and I have no idea." But, he continued, there have been plenty of unusual instances of objects reappearing at his store after he sold them—not in a mystical way, but strange nonetheless. For instance, he'd sell an object and sometime later someone else would bring it back. He'd resell it, and again someone else would bring it back. "Objects that seem to have spirit attachments create problems for the owners of the objects," said paranormal researcher and expert Rosemary Ellen Guiley in her book *The Encyclopedia of Ghosts and Spirits*. "Possessed possessions can be any object: clothing, jewelry, furniture, household goods, machines, artwork, religious items, photographs, stones, other natural objects, and so forth. . . . The ability of spirits to inhabit objects is known universally in magical systems."

Alien Lights over Portland

Similar to ghost tales, there seems never to be a dearth of stories about alien encounters, UFO sightings, and even alien abductions. Look up at the night sky sometime when you're outside, preferably in a place where there's no light pollution and the Milky Way looks milky. Perhaps you'll see something strange overhead. If nothing else, you'll be awed by the spectacle of shimmering stars in an expansive universe.

Residents saw more than fireworks light up the night sky over Portland on July 4, 2013. According to a news report by KATU television reporter Erica Nochlin, several lights were seen in the skies over the waterfront before the city's fireworks show. Nochlin, as a good reporter, asked area residents what they believed the lights may have been. As expected, the responses varied from serious to humorous.

"Aliens, it had to be aliens," said one man. "What are those, fireflies?" asked a little boy. The simplest, and seemingly most correct answer, came from a woman who said simply, "UFO."

The news station also posted the question on its Facebook page, and user response was just as varied. One person joked that it was Iron Man, another said it was a drone, and yet another said it was probably just a satellite. One man wrote that the footage he saw from the news station was not unlike other UFO footage he had seen. One flaw in these reader responses is that they refer to the lights as the singular "it," when in actuality there were three lights recorded in the sky. The brightest light remained stationary, another was dim and looked as if it were blinking out, and a third moved slowly and silently beneath the other two lights, first to the west and then back toward the east.

Nochlin, in an effort to get to the bottom of the story, talked to Jim Todd, the director of Space Science Education at the Oregon Museum of Science and Industry, who said the lights were likely nothing more than sky lanterns that some residents claimed to have released that very night from a party in their backyard. "Based on what we've been told, it's not moving much at all and it appears to be kind of drifting," Todd told Nochlin. "It's probably a sky lantern—I'm pretty confident that it is."

He said the lights were too slow to be either a satellite or a space station, and that if they were planes or helicopters there should have been noise associated with them, but there were no sounds. Others who are inclined to believe beings from the outer limits are interested in us, however, tend to believe the lights were more than manmade objects. Even Todd, after saying the lights were most likely sky lanterns, still referred to them as UFOs, Nochlin said in her report because "we can't be 100 percent sure."

The strange lights on the Fourth of July weren't the only recent instance of potential UFO activity in the area. One Oregon resident, while driving home around 9:30 P.M. on March 17, 2013, noticed something unusual in the otherwise clear skies over Portland. A cluster of four "bright orange lights" were "floating" and "jumping" around in the sky, the witness reported to the National UFO

Reporting Center. "They appeared to be moving together but not connected," the witness explained. They moved slowly, similar to hot air balloons, but in a controlled pattern for about thirty minutes. Some would "rotate around others."

The witness stopped at an intersection, where more sky was visible, and was surprised when he saw many more of the same lights. He estimated there was about thirty of them. Others, he learned later, reported having seen fifty or more of them earlier in the evening. When the witness reached his apartment, he realized he wasn't seeing things that weren't there. Patrons at a local bar and grill were outside, their heads turned upward to look at the unfamiliar objects.

The witness said the lights were unlike anything he'd seen before. "Eventually, they faded into the distance as they all moved west and disappeared into the night sky," he said.

Like so many UFO sightings, it is unknown what these people saw. Though they had never before seen lights act the way these apparently did, could it still have been something earthly and explainable, perhaps a late-night balloon festival? Or did these Portlanders witness something out of this world?

A twenty-seven-year-old woman claims that ten years earlier, in the early hours of August 20, 2003, she saw actual beings from the outer limits. She shared her experience with the UFO Watch website, saying she encountered tall, grayish figures with round heads and long arms and legs. The woman does not give background to the sighting, such as where in Portland she was or what she was doing, but described the creatures' spaceship as "dark and gloomy" with "no lights." Not recounting the details of her alleged abduction, the woman explained that after her experience she noticed a strange mark on the back of her head and saw a "strange white light" in the sky for days after the event, a light she claims nobody in her presence could see but her.

Again, what is the reality of the woman's claims? Stories like these have to stand on their own merit, and it's left up to the reader to believe or disbelieve. Where you stand on these likely depends on your own encounters with the unexplained. Chances are, if you've experienced a paranormal occurrence, you're more likely to believe in extraterrestrials and the like.

But there is one theory that says aliens really are not what they seem to be. They are not creatures from other worlds, but rather demons from other spheres. Alien abductions, some claim, are attacks by demonic entities—or fallen angels—that try to fool and oppress their human victims.

A Witch's Castle

An old, decrepit-looking building in Portland's Forest Park very much resembles a castle in shambles. Over the years, it has become a popular place for teenagers and young adults to hang out, often bringing with them the spirits of a less paranormal kind (the type that will make their heads buzz). They don't need to drink whiskey and beer, however, to encounter the presence of a witch that is said to inhabit the broken castle and surrounding forest.

The witch's story starts in about 1850, when a man named Danford Balch filed a claim for the land in question and, after securing the property, hired a transient worker from Fort Vancouver, Washington, named Mortimer Stump. Because of his dire circumstances, the tramp wound up living with the family—Balch and his wife, Mary Jane, and their nine children—which added another mouth to an already full dinner table. As the days moved on, turning into weeks and months, Stump, a lonely fellow, began to be affectionate toward one of Balch's daughters, fifteen-year-old Anna. The tale doesn't reveal how old Stump was, but it is assumed there was quite a span of years between him and young Anna. That, however, didn't stop the collision course upon which the two had set themselves. The feelings must have been mutual, because when Stump asked Balch if he could marry his daughter, Anna fought for the cause as well. Balch, in an effort to protect his daughter from marrying an older man and one without much economic promise, said no. The discussion apparently became so heated that Balch threatened Stump, telling him that if he married his daughter behind his back, he would seek revenge and kill him. The couple, either truly in love or determined to not be bullied by Anna's parents, moved ahead with their wedding plans. One day, after packing and preparing, Stump and Anna left for Stump's land claim across the Willamette River, northeast of present-day St. Johns, and eloped.

As might be expected from such a story, Balch eventually carried out his promise to Stump. Ironically, however, it was Balch's wife, Mary Jane, who goaded her husband to go through with the evil deed. Sometime after their marriage, the couple known as Mr. and Mrs. Stump returned to Portland for supplies, and while there ran into Anna's parents. Mary Jane, playing devil's advocate, urged her husband to kill their unwanted son-in-law. Balch pumped the shotgun he had nearby, took aim at Stump's face, and pulled the trigger, killing the man instantly and leaving his young daughter a widow. It was a crime for which Anna could not forgive her parents.

During his trial, Balch said he acted outside his own volition, claiming his wife had put a curse on him that caused him to kill Stump. We don't know much about Balch's wife or why he suggested that she had cursed him, but there must have been reason for him to say that. He was either trying to excuse his deed, or Mary Jane had been practicing witchcraft. No matter—Balch eventually got his due. He was sent to jail, later escaped, was arrested again, and was hanged for his crime on October 17, 1859.

Balch's life ends there, but the witch's story does not. Balch's land eventually was divided among his children, while Mary Jane continued to live in the couple's cabin. As time marched on, the land was used by several owners and eventually was given to the city of Portland by Donald MacLeay in 1897. Not far from the Balch cabin, a stone structure was built in the 1950s as a ranger station with restrooms for visitors to the park. Time took its toll on the building, however, and it eventually deteriorated and was left abandoned except for the teenagers and ghosts that supposedly roam here. It is this building, built on land once owned by the alleged witch Mary Jane Balch, that resembles a castle.

Orbs, strange lights, and dark shades have been seen in the area. There is also supposedly a strange battle between spirits that on occasion appear out of nowhere at midnight, dressed in battle gear and waging war on each other on the battlefront that is, according to lore, the witch's property—or Mary Jane's, if indeed she was a witch at all. If this is true, it appears the feud that started more than 150 years ago in this otherwise peaceful forest in Portland still continues in the netherworld, where the Balch family and Mr. and Mrs. Mortimer Stump now reside. Apparently death and the passing of decades have done little to assuage the contention between the two clans. Sheez, why can't we all just get along!

The Angry Spirit of Forest Grove

This next story sounds like a folktale to me, but I find it rather interesting. According to the tale, the specter of an angry man lurks in the dense woods near Forest Grove in Washington County and is attributed with causing several deaths. How does he dispatch his victims? Why, by beating them to a pulp, of course.

Forest Grove, a city with a population of about twenty-two thousand by 2012 estimates, was settled by European immigrants—the first of whom were Alvin and Abigail Smith—in the 1840s. Before they arrived, however, the area was inhabited by the Tualatin branch of the Kalapuya Indians. The Smith family was soon joined by the Clark and Littlejohn families, along with others, and by 1845 the town, known at the time as West Tualatin Plains, numbered fifteen families. That was just the beginning, as more good things were to come for the area soon to be known as Forest Grove. A school for children and a home for orphans were established in 1849; the first railroad was established in 1869; and the city was formally incorporated in 1872.

According to lore, some people who've entered the woods later came out looking the worse for wear with bruises on their skin. When asked what happened, they said they were attacked by an unseen presence. If their stories are true, it appears Forest Grove is haunted by a mysterious phantom that for some reason holds a grudge against those who trespass into its wooded realm.

As with all places of note, there are many things that make up the history and flair of Forest Grove. The best way to get an understanding of it is to visit, but even then you might not come to fully understand the ghost tale associated with its woods. While it is true, according to paranormal investigators, that spirits can sometimes harm human beings, it is difficult for many reasons to track the superstition that a spirit kills people in the woods. For one thing, it's hard to arrest and charge a ghost for a crime. No arrest means a cold case or, in this case, a possible folktale.

Ghost Boat of the Willamette River

There sits a book on my library shelf, a small gray-and-white paperback that I take down every once in a while to reread the captivating stories between its covers. The book, *Ghost Ships: True Stories of Nautical Nightmares, Hauntings, and Disasters* by Richard Winer (who also wrote the popular *The Devil's Triangle*), is just one of many publications on the alleged mysteries behind some of the world's most renowned and haunted ships. The ghost boat of the Willamette River is not among the stories in Winer's book, but it is a tale that is popular among those who know Oregon's haunted history best.

The river itself, like most bodies of water, has a long history that, if I were to write about it all, would fill volumes. In brief, the Willamette River, one of Oregon's best-known rivers, lies entirely in northwest Oregon and is a major tributary of the Columbia River. Its main stem is 187 miles long. It flows northward between the Oregon Coast Range and the Cascade Range. The river and its tributaries form the Willamette Valley, and Portland surrounds the river's mouth at the Columbia. Created by plate tectonics about 3.5 million years ago, it later was altered by volcanic activity and erosion, while the river's drainage basin was modified by the Missoula Floods at the end of the last ice age. Indigenous peoples to the Willamette Valley are the Chinook, Clackamas, and Kalapuya, who all subsisted on the river's salmon and trout. British lieutenant William Robert Broughton of the Vancouver Expedition (1791–95), a diplomatic expedition led by George Vancouver, reached the river in 1792 and later wrote about it in his journal. Soon thereafter, the fur trade started in the area and lasted through much of the nineteenth century. William Clark of Lewis and Clark fame entered the Willamette from the Columbia in April 1806 while on the Corps of Discovery Expedition, after having first passed the river's mouth while on the Columbia earlier.

Over the course of recent years, there has been a lot of development on or near the river, including bridges and dams, adding more chapters to the history of the area. The river today is visited by thousands of people who use it for boating, fishing, and other recreational and leisure activities.

And if the legend is true, there appears at unexpected times the image of a ghost ship, which moves not quite silently across the water. Its foghorn has been heard by some wary and startled witnesses. Those hornlike wailing sounds get to people every time, causing consternation and a little uneasiness. The sounds, heard by several individuals, led to discussion on one online blog, where visitors described the noise as "long and deep," "really haunting," "a sorrowful wailing," and much like how one would imagine a "ghost train" might sound. The train theory might not be too far off. One blogger said she believes the sound is indeed a foghorn, coming from a train bridge near Kelley Point Park in northwest Portland. But then again, perhaps the answer lies farther away, in the spirit world from whence the horn reveals itself only once in a while to unsuspecting victims.

Once the horn sounds, catching the attention of its mortal witnesses, the ship and its unearthly occupants slowly fade into oblivion as if they never existed. This sparks at least one question with me. If the story is true, it appears that not only people and animals can appear as spirit images, but also inanimate objects. But how can an inanimate object, something that has never lived or breathed, appear as a spirit image? This question, prevalent among those who study the paranormal, is perhaps one of the more difficult to answer. There are countless instances of ghost ships, aircraft, automobiles, and even trains. One story in my book *Haunted Idaho* tells about a house that, at unexpected times, would appear to startled passersby on the very block where it once stood. Lights would shine from within, just as they did in the mortal sphere, and human cries would be heard emanating from the phantom house. But the physical house no longer existed. It was razed years before, after a violent crime was committed there.

One theory is that such apparitions are not actual manifestations of physical energy, but rather mirages or prerecorded impressions, similar to a residual haunting but manifested by different laws. That's at least one explanation for the ghost boat of the Willamette, though there might be other theories out there, some not explored. No matter. If you see the ghost boat or hear the deathly wail of its foghorn, you've just experienced the paranormal, perhaps coming quite close to the next sphere of existence.

The Not-So-Amusing Ghosts

For most visitors, amusement parks are places where fun comes alive. Carousels, fun houses, games, Ferris wheels, roller coasters, and cotton candy are just some of the things that make these places memorable for both the young and the young at heart. For a few disheartened souls, however, amusement parks are anything but amusing. Sometimes they are places that, far from one's intents and thoughts, turn into places of cruelty and sadness. Is that what happened for one young boy who, more than three decades ago, visited Oaks Amusement Park in southeast Portland? We can only guess what happened to him and why his spirit lingers behind.

The spirit that is seen here, according to lore, is that of a young child dressed in 1970s garb. For at least a couple of decades, he has appeared to unsuspecting visitors at different places in the park before quickly vanishing. We do not know to whom this spirit belongs or why it is attached to the park. Perhaps the boy died here, the victim of an accident. Or, for all we know, he died of natural causes and only visits the park as a ghost because in life it was one of his favorite places to play. Spirits are known to attach themselves not only to places where they might have died, but also to locations that brought them happiness in mortality.

The amusement park has brought excitement to many people over the past hundred-plus years since it was built in 1890. The park that sits near Sellwood Bridge today has around two dozen rides open seasonally, a skating rink open all year, and cozy picnic grounds. When visiting the park, there's no doubt you'll have a fun time. Just be mindful if you come across a young boy dressed to look like someone from *The Brady Bunch* and whose body isn't a solid form but instead more like a wisp of fog. Chances are it's the apparition of a once-living little boy who still likes to have fun at the park.

For a couple of other ghost children, Jantzen Beach Amusement Park, which was popular from its opening day on May 26, 1928, was a place of excitement and fun. Located on 123 acres at Hayden Island in northern Portland, it was the largest amusement park in the country at the time. The price of admission was ten cents and granted access to a swimming pool, Ferris wheel, and the Big Dipper, a large roller coaster that was the park's main attraction. It also had a fun house that contained "The Laughing Lady," a Hall of Mirrors, animated ghosts and goblins, a swinging bridge, and a turntable. Jantzen Beach was a fun venue that attracted people from far and wide, and children and young adults considered it one of the best places in the Pacific Northwest. The park closed in September 1970; today the site is home to a shopping mall called the Jantzen Beach SuperCenter, where the park's carousel now resides.

While the park no longer exists, a shade of its earthly presence does. At least a couple of children still have fond attachments to the carousel. It is rumored that the spirits of a boy and girl have been seen using the merry-go-round when no one else was aboard. They always seem happy, as if they're having the time of their immortal lives, but in the midst of their fun they'll sometimes turn their heads and gaze into the distance as if looking for someone, maybe their mother calling to them. Or maybe they're just watching the mortal crowd as it wanders past.

Portland's Haunted Schools

Some of the things that spark a haunting are the emotional ties individuals might have to a place, whether it's a house, business, or a church. Something highly emotional or traumatic—such as the person's demise—could have happened there, but it need not always be the imprint of death that lingers. Oftentimes it is the imprint of life, which itself is full of emotions, from happiness to excitement.

A happy home life might imprint those feelings on the space-time continuum. A place of business where a devoted worker spent much of his or her waking time may be a place the spirit visits once it has departed from the mortal realm. A church building, where strong beliefs were shared, might be imprinted with the parishioner's faith. And a schoolhouse, where for many weeks out of the year anxious and eager students spent most of their days in classrooms, crowded hallways, cafeterias, and gymnasiums, may be filled with a frenzy of residual emotions. Schools often are some of the most haunted places for these reasons and others. Oregon allegedly has a number of haunted schoolhouses, and a few of them are in Portland.

A strange partial or headless apparition is believed to haunt Roosevelt High School, which opened to the public in 1921. The spirit supposedly belongs to a male student, who some believe might have taken his own life many years ago. As with urban legends, however, there's not much more to tell about the story except that the boy's spirit will show itself to unsuspecting witnesses when they least expect it. Don't worry—this spirit has not turned malicious toward anybody else . . . except, of course, to scare them with his headless form.

The former Kennedy School, an elementary school in northwest Portland that was open from 1915 to 1975, is supposedly visited by the spirit of a woman in the restroom. The facility, which is now owned by the McMenamin family as a hotel and restaurant, doesn't sound so creepy, however. The hotel offers some rooms that still feature the old school's chalkboards and cloakrooms. Others are decorated with authors' themes. Another unique feature is the old school's auditorium, where guests can still enjoy a movie.

Marshall High School allegedly has spirits that call out names of late-night workers. Rumor has it that janitors who've worked in the building heard their names called out when no one else was around. They'd hear noises, as if other people were inside, but when they went to a room to investigate they'd find it empty. Are these the sounds of past students or teachers? And who are the ghosts that know the janitors' names?

The University of Portland, established in 1901, is rumored to be haunted by several ghosts, some of which date back to the school's earliest days. University Commons, located on Waud's Bluff, is supposedly haunted by a cranky spirit belonging to a man named Frank Houston, a farmer who lived and worked in the area before the school was built. He turned down offers to sell his land to the school, but once he passed away his wife relented and sold the property. His spirit is said to haunt the campus, showing up at places where a fence marked his property line. His spirit never stays around for long, however, for once you catch a glimpse of ol' Frank, the apparition slowly fades back into the netherworld from whence it came.

The university's Mago Hunt Theater is rumored to be haunted by the spirit of a woman dressed in Victorian garb. Others have reported feeling unnerved whenever they're near Waud's Bluff at night, and doors in Franz Hall supposedly open and close on their own. It is unknown to whom these spirits belong, but they seem to have an attachment to the old school campus, so they were likely former students, teachers, or staff.

Ghosts chasing other ghosts allegedly have been seen on the Lewis and Clark College campus. To whom these spirits belong and why the midnight chase ensues is anybody's guess, but apparently it's not the only creepy thing that happens here. It is said phantom screaming can sometimes be heard echoing throughout the campus, coming not from a physical location on the school grounds but rather from the netherworld where the running specters return.

Friendly Haunted Hotels

There's a scene in the movie *1408*, based on a short story found in Stephen King's collection *Everything's Eventual*, in which paranormal writer Mike Enslin (played by John Cusack) winds up staying in the grandiose but spooky Dolphin Hotel. The hotel, for superstitious reasons, has no thirteenth floor; it does have a fourteenth floor, however, and one room on that level is haunted by something evil. The entity, whatever it is—perhaps even the very room itself—toys with both Enslin's sanity and his life. At one point while in room 1408, Enslin turns on his recorder and says to it, looking around the spacious room: "Hotel rooms are a naturally creepy place. . . . How many people have slept in that bed before you? How many of them were sick? How many of them lost their minds? How many of them . . . died?"

If nothing else, this fictional story offers some food for thought and strikes a very real chord about why hotels are supposedly some of a city's most haunted places. Nothing as drastic as what is portrayed in *1408* ever occurred at hotels in Portland, but several of them have stories of ghosts that just won't go away.

Voted Portland's best hotel in 2012 by the *Oregonian*, The Benson is an elaborate building that many of the rich and famous have visited over the years, including several U.S. presidents. Built in 1913 at Southwest Broadway and Oak Street in downtown Portland, the hotel is elegantly designed and includes two spacious ballrooms, fourteen floors, 287 rooms, and if you ask the right people, at least a few ghosts.

Hotel guests have reported seeing the spirits of both adults and children. It is said that most of the activity happened during renovation, though stories exist about paranormal activity in the building at other times as well. One visitor claims on Yelp.com that the spirit of a small child approached her on the ninth floor. She posted her experience on the website, asking if anyone had information as to whom the spirit might belong. As of this writing, the post had not received a definitive answer.

Other stories include guests seeing the shade of a man walking down the grand staircase from the mezzanine before fading from view, and a gentleman ghost who sits at a table in one of the downtown restaurants.

If you're looking for luxury and a little R&R, try the Heathman Hotel in downtown Portland. Built in 1927, the hotel is independently owned today and, much to my delight, "boasts one of the few catalogued lending hotel libraries in the country," according to its website. Check out a good book and relax in the lounge or in your room. At least a few of the hotel's 150 rooms are considered by some to be haunted.

According to one online source, the rooms that have numbers ending in 03 have strange things that happen in them. Guests have claimed to see apparitions in certain rooms, noticed that personal items have been misplaced or used when no one else was in the room, and felt unseen presences nearby. There doesn't appear to be anything malicious in this remarkable venue. It's likely that the spirits, much like their human counterparts, enjoy staying at the beautiful Heathman. It's just that sometimes the two worlds—ours and theirs—run into each other.

In some circles, the White Eagle Saloon & Hotel is considered to be the most haunted hotel in Portland. Built in 1899, the White Eagle today hosts nightly musical performances, helping it become known as the area's "rock 'n roll" hotel. The building, with its eleven original guest rooms, has been deemed by the Travel Channel to be "one of the spookiest watering holes in the country."

The hotel allegedly is haunted by the spirit of a disgruntled house worker named Sam. Visitors claim to have felt presences in their rooms at night, sometimes like unseen hands pressing on them to the point that it becomes difficult to get out of bed. Toilet paper in the women's restroom has been known to fly off the rollers, chairs move of their own volition, and doors close when no one is nearby to push them. Hotel visitors also have said they've heard strange sounds such as crying, moaning, and phantom footsteps. One spirit, dubbed "Barney," supposedly walks the main floor and sometimes visits the basement.

Paranormal Activity at the Falcon Apartments

I've lived in a couple of apartments in my time with rooms that were anything but friendly. If nothing else, they seemed melancholy and disturbed, as if unseen presences had made them their abode. Walking into the rooms gave me a sense that I was the uninvited guest, not the unseen entities. My imagination would get the best of me at these times, and I'd wonder what might have happened in the rooms to cause me such uncomfortable feelings. That's the thing about living in places where others have lived before you. What went on in those places before you arrived? What spirits did the former tenants invite—on purpose or inadvertently—to live with them?

Of course, some places just naturally have an aura about them that might strike imaginative feelings of otherworldly presences. A room without a lot of natural light, for instance, might look dark and melancholy, thus prompting our own ill feelings of "what if?" According to stories about the Falcon Apartments, located at 5415 North Albina Avenue in Portland, however, it's not ill-lit rooms or other creepy auras that spark the ghost tales, but rather alleged actual sightings of supernatural elements from beyond the grave.

At least two spirits are rumored to haunt the apartments, but they have never been seen together, leading to the assumption that their alleged mortal passings happened independently of each other. The spirits, at different times, have been reportedly seen in the hallways, manager's office, and even next to the mailboxes. Both allegedly appear to be older gentlemen. One of them is believed to be a Mr. Cook, who liked to fix the mailboxes whenever something went cockeyed. He'd sit in his big white chair, facing the boxes, and watch the crowd pass by. That is where his spirit has been seen—still sitting in his white chair. The other spirit, known only as James, is typically seen wandering the hallways and other places inside the apartment complex.

Residual Sounds of a Brutal Crime

The teenage years, even with all of their high school stresses and peer pressure, are supposed to be a happy time in a growing person's life. It's a time of learning, making friends, and setting a course for the future. The future of one fifteen-year-old Portland girl, however, was annihilated by the evil intents of a demented psychopath more than half a century ago.

The year was 1949. Thelma Taylor was waiting at a bus stop on North Fessenden Street so she could get to her work, picking berries in the country. Instead, she was picked up by a man with other plans for young Thelma. He took her to St. John's Bridge, which spans the Willamette River in Portland, and there, according to the story, bound and raped her. He kept her as his prisoner for almost a week before she died. The man was arrested, charged, and eventually received the death sentence for his crimes. His evil deeds, however, seem to live on in a residual haunting of the traumatic episode.

It's not uncommon for local police to receive calls in the summer—around the same time that Thelma apparently was abducted—because of screams for help coming from the area near the bridge. Police respond, only to find the place empty.

Visit the area and see if you can hear the unearthly screams of now-deceased Thelma. They won't be pretty sounds if you hear them, but ones that will make your skin crawl. They apparently will be so believable that you too might be inclined to call the local police.

The Shade of a Ghostly Reader

Whoever said reading was just for us mortals? Apparently, there's a shade of a man who likes to sit on the second floor of the North Portland Library. He hasn't been seen by human eyes, but his form is picked up by digital monitors inside the library. First noticed on the monitors in 1990, he was thereafter seen many times throughout the ensuing years, though not as often as of late.

When the library attendant first noticed the image on a monitor, she walked up to the second floor to tell the man he should not be up there. It was a closed portion of the library at the time and under renovation. When the attendant reached the second floor, she saw the table and chairs where the man had sat, but the room was empty. She walked back down the stairs and again noticed the same image on the computer monitor: the shade of a man sitting motionless at the table. Soon, because he was often seen on the monitors but never face-to-face, library staff named the apparition "The Man Upstairs."

It is not known to whom the shade belongs or why it visits the library. Perhaps he was a library patron in mortal life and still has a fond attachment to the building and its many printed volumes. If so, maybe he'll find this very one you're holding in your hands and be surprised that his story made it into a book. If you are lucky enough to see him, ask for his autograph.

Northwest
Oregon

SPIRITS RUN FREELY THROUGHOUT THE NORTHWEST PART OF THE STATE, attesting that Oregon's hauntings are not confined to its largest city. This section covers stories from the city of Astoria south to Lincoln and Benton Counties, east to Linn County, and north to Multnomah County, making a nice square in the upper left of the state. This is a scenic block of Oregon Country that has a mix of modernity and old times. There's plenty of history in this region, including places that Meriwether Lewis and William Clark visited during their famous Corps of Discovery Expedition. Later, pioneers on the Oregon Trail would reach their journey's end here in the scenic coastal West. You'll read about the ghosts that haunt an old lighthouse and iconic beaches, the mummy character that roams a section of the Oregon Coast, the ghost of a warlock, UFO sightings, and much more. Welcome to Northwest Oregon, where the climate is moderate, the scenery is beautiful, and the ghosts are many.

The Curse of Tillamook Lighthouse

Rain fell in torrents on a night in 1880 as lightning streaked the darkened sky. Ocean waves crested high, making it difficult for the captains to steer their small boats to shore. Where, exactly, was the harbor? The storm forced the vessels—several of them throughout

the night—upon the rocks or under the water. By morning, witnesses saw the eerie scene: small fishing boats broken to pieces or tipped over amid the crashing waves. In all, twenty-five people died.

At first glance, it appeared to be a natural disaster, but some people thought something more sinister was at work. Some believed the disaster was caused by the evil spirits that, according to local Indians at the time, inhabited the jagged rocks near the shores of Cannon Beach. If the Tillamook Lighthouse had been working, perhaps at least some of the wrecks could have been averted, but construction was still underway on the island rock the lighthouse sits upon today. Without the light to combat the darkness, the alleged spirits had full sway of the area and the boats that came to port.

To deepen the mystery, stories of spooks in the area did not end once the lighthouse was completed. The lighthouse itself, located a little more than a mile offshore from Tillamook Head, became a focus of some of these ghostly tales. Lightkeepers, for instance, reported hearing strange groans on the stairwell when no one else was inside. Were these the evil spirits making themselves manifest to the cliffs' new arrivals, warning them that they were treading cursed land?

Whatever entities lurk the cliffsides or the surf at Tillamook Rock, they apparently have been there for a while. During the storm of 1880, witnesses to the disaster reported seeing a ghost ship make its way through the wreckage. Some believed it was picking up the souls of the dead. The ghost ship allegedly was seen again in the 1950s by a Coast Guard crew. The ship, the crew reported, broke through dense fog just below the lighthouse and then vanished into thin air.

The Ghost Ship of Siletz Bay

Farther south from Tillamook is Siletz Bay, located in south Lincoln City, where another ghost ship—or perhaps several—reportedly has been seen over the years by many different witnesses. The phantom vessel, with its sails set, has been observed making its way across the water to some unknown, ephemeral destination. Those who see it never know if it ever makes its journey's end, however, because the ship suddenly vanishes as quickly as it appears. We do not know for sure the name of this phantom ship, though there have been some guesses pertaining to its identity, and apparently there is good reason why it appears in the area. "Legends and reports of ghostly ships are universal," writes Rosemary Ellen Guiley in *The Encyclopedia of Ghosts and Spirits.* "Most are linked to disasters and shipwrecks. Phantom ships usually appear at the scene of the disaster and may reenact their wrecks, especially on stormy nights."

There have been several shipwrecks over the years in the bay. The remnants of one disaster—perhaps the wreck of the 100-foot 1860s brig *Blanco,* which was buried in the mudflats—were still visible until the 1980s. The *Blanco,* it is believed, drifted into the bay bottom side up in 1864. Other ships that have reportedly made the bay their graveyard are the schooner *Sunbeam,* which disappeared in the 1880s; the 113-ton schooner *Uncle John,* lost off Cape Foulweather in 1876; and the *Phoebe Fay,* which became stranded north of Cape Foulweather in 1883. Is it the *Blanco* that every once in a while is seen sailing on ethereal waves at Siletz Bay, or is it one of these other vessels? Perhaps it's all of them, seen at different times by different witnesses. Or maybe it is none of them, and the phantom ship is some other unknown vessel that haunts the waters.

Whatever the identity of the phantom ship, it apparently was a big scare to a local resident, who, according to one online story, claimed she saw the ghostly vessel move straight and fast across the water toward her house. Luckily it was just an apparition, because if it had been the real thing and hadn't vanished before hitting the woman's house, it would have done some serious damage.

Some years ago, an elderly woman who worked at the North Lincoln County Historical Museum claimed to have seen a large schooner roll across the bay one day when she looked out the window. By the time she rushed downstairs to tell others to look at the mysterious ship—vessels that large no longer make their way into the bay—it had disappeared, Anne Hall, the museum's executive director, told me.

Today, Siletz Bay is a scenic spot along Oregon's northwestern coast and a popular place for crabbing. The crustaceans are most active several hours after low tide, but there are plenty of other things to do here too, such as beachcombing, kite flying, and whale watching. There's even an activity called tidepooling, which involves visiting the rocky intertidal zones and searching for the many different kinds of organisms in shallow pools that high tide carries to shore. You might want to bring a camera, because you never know what you might find. It could come in handy if you spot any ghost ships, their sails still set, drifting across the waves.

The Sea Serpents of Newport

The lifespan of an octopus is around five years, while some sharks might live for thirty years. Gray whales can live for around sixty years, blue whales for ninety years, and the bowhead whale for more than two hundred years. That's a long time to stay under water, and it makes a person wonder how much of the world's oceans such a long-living mammal sees in its lifetime.

The expansive ocean is home to abundant sea life that scientists still are discovering in one form or another. In a single two-year period, from 2010 to 2012, *National Geographic Daily News* articles reported a variety of unique findings. In 2010, scientists discovered giant craters "spewing fresh water and brimming with bacteria" at the bottom of the Dead Sea, and also found ten potentially new species during a six-week expedition in the Atlantic Ocean, including the rare basket star known as the Star of the Deep. And in 2012, *National Geographic* reported: "Several species of previously unknown marine animals have been discovered thriving in one of the strangest habitats on Earth—next to hydrothermal vents on the ocean floor near Antarctica, in an environment that is too hot, too dark, and too toxic to support most other sea life."

If fascinating new species like these are still being discovered, couldn't there indeed be such things as sea serpents? And if so, how long would such beings live? Are the strange, unknown creatures allegedly seen in the world's oceans today ancient monsters, or have they only been around a short time? We'll never know unless a sea monster is captured and studied, but like Bigfoot and other elusive creatures of legend and lore, it is unlikely that such a creature will ever be caught. They will, for the most part, remain in tall tales and stories of the strange and unexplained, like one story that dates back to 1935.

It was a simpler time back then, one without the Internet, smart-phones, and social media. What it did have were the grapevine and a community newspaper—and so the story was shared of a man and woman who claimed to have seen a couple of sea monsters in the ocean's surf at Seal Rock near Newport.

The couple said they in fact had seen many different monsters that looked as if they came straight out of a science-fiction story. As the tale goes, printed in the June 13, 1935, issue of the *Yaquina Bay News*, the husband and wife heard the noisy goings-on of what they thought were sea lions and went outside to see what the animals were doing. When they stepped outside, though, they didn't see any playful sea lions. Instead, they noticed a large creature they could only describe as a sea serpent frolicking in the surf. Then the couple noticed the beast wasn't alone; another similar creature also was in the water.

The one they could see most clearly they described as being forty to sixty feet long, according to the newspaper article, with a head as long as a man and at least three feet wide. One of the creatures seemed to be enjoying itself in the water, until it finally tired of its game and headed south. The other creature would surface here and there but didn't make much commotion at all. Eventually, it also disappeared.

Some people believe the story is completely fabricated, told to help spark more tourism in the area, as such stories usually do. But, knowing there are many creatures still undiscovered in the ocean depths, what if the couple's claims were true, and they really did see two sea monsters playing in their watery home on the Oregon coast?

The Monster of Devil's Lake

The man gazed out to sea from his beachside home, not expecting to see anything extraordinary, but he did. Strange movement at the water's edge drew his attention: long yellow arms—tentacles—reached out of the surf and groped the beach. The tentacles, "thick as a man's thigh" at their widest point, were all that the man saw. But once they slipped under the water again, large movement on the surface attested that the creature, whatever it was, was moving beneath. Stan Allyn waited four years after the sighting, so strange was it, before he told anyone. It was not the first time that someone claimed to see a serpent-like creature in Lincoln County's Devil's Lake.

Early Native Americans who occupied the area told stories of a giant fish or some other water creature that would rise to the surface, startling fishermen and causing consternation among tribesmen. The lake, which has a surface area of around 680 acres, is managed today by the Devil's Lake Water Improvement District. Once you learn the lake's depth, you might find it difficult to believe that anything larger than overgrown catfish or carp can inhabit the water. The lake has been reported to be around twenty-one feet at its deepest point. Some fishermen have reported that their fish finders detect large movement under the water, and every now and again these fish tales become whoppers. There are plenty of mysteries on Planet Earth, as well as in its many waters, and it seems the monster of Devil's Lake is one of them.

There is, however, nothing mysterious about the nearly two-ton artist's rendering of the alleged creature that greets visitors at the entrance of Regatta Grounds Park on West Devil's Lake Road. Commissioned by the Public Arts Committee, Heidi Erickson and Doug Kroger worked for more than two years to fabricate the "Devil's Lake Creature" from recycled metal and rubber retread material. The finished product was a thirteen-foot-tall, eighteen-foot-long silver dinosaur-like emblem that, since its placement at the site, has been a major draw for children who like to climb the creature.

While the sculpture helped to interest children in both the art and math behind its construction, it suffered plenty of wear and tear from being treated like a jungle gym. Officials finally fenced off the statue and placed a "Danger: Restricted Area" sign nearby.

It's not every day a monster is honored with a statue of its own. If the many-tentacled creature knew what attention it drew above the water's surface, it might emerge more frequently; instead, sightings of the alleged creature have diminished over the years. The statue still stands, but what happened to the real monster? Some believe it may have exited the lake the same way it entered— through the D River that runs through Lincoln City.

No danger sign warns visitors about the allegedly real monster that inhabits the lake, though, so consider this story warning enough. Think twice before going near the water, just in case the stories are true and there really is something monstrous beneath the surface.

The Haunting of Fort Clatsop

For nearly five months after reaching the Pacific Ocean, members of the Corps of Discovery Expedition, led by Meriwether Lewis and William Clark, stayed at a little place they named after the Clatsop Indians. They had reached the Pacific Ocean in November 1805, taking more than a year to cross the country. Eighteen months prior, they had left Camp Wood, Illinois, at the mouth of the Missouri River, and had traveled 3,700 miles to Cape Disappointment in present-day Washington, where they caught their first glimpse of the western ocean. Their objective, commissioned by President Thomas Jefferson, was to search the backcountry of the western United States in an effort to document the "face of the country."

It was too late in the year for them to make the journey home, as Old Man Winter would make travel difficult and dangerous. Instead, they tarried in the place they named Fort Clatsop near present-day Astoria, building a fort that was just fifty square feet, not roomy for the thirty-four persons and one dog it housed. They made good use of the space, however, by having parallel cabins. One cabin contained three rooms for the enlisted men's quarters; the other contained the captains' room, a family room, an orderly room, and a storeroom. The space between the facing cabins formed a parade ground, with gates installed at each end.

The men lived in their temporary home, which they began to build on December 9 shortly after their arrival in Cape Disappointment, from December 25, 1805, to March 23, 1806, when they started their journey homeward. It was a pleasant spot that provided an abundance of food in the form of wildlife, especially elk. It was also the first American military structure built west of the Rocky Mountains.

Expedition members passed the winter with a routine of chores—trading for fish and vegetables, hunting elk, and stitching more than three hundred pairs of moccasins—while the rain fell steadily. According to one member of the expedition, Patrick Gass, the group had its full share of rain during their visit to the Pacific

Northwest. The promise of returning home to a more sedate and less watery clime looked appealing. "From the 4th of November 1805 to the 25th of March 1806," he wrote in the spring of 1806, "there were not more than twelve days in which it did not rain, and of these but six were clear."

Rain still is abundant in upper Oregon, helping to create the lush beauty that exists here today. But unlike rainy days in some other parts of the country, it does not keep people from being busy. Nor did the near-constant rain during the winter of 1805–06 keep the explorers from being busy. It is said they used their time documenting the many things they had seen and experienced.

"Thomas Jefferson had instructed Lewis to record 'the soil & face of the country,' the animals, and the customs, food and clothing of the American Indian nations," the National Park Service website states. "To this end, Lewis and Clark made good use of their time at Fort Clatsop. Lewis prepared detailed notes on more than 30 mammals, birds and plants not previously described by science. His observations are still valued by researchers today. Clark used data collected on the journey, including celestial observations, to complete a map of their route from Fort Mandan to Fort Clatsop—an invaluable tool for later travelers." They also traded with the area's Indians, the Clatsop Nation. The Indians were, of course, familiar with European traders, having already met many who had ventured to the area for their own purposes. But the Corps of Discovery was the first group to stay so long among the natives. For the most part, they developed friendly relations with each other, and when the expedition members took up their journey again on March 23, 1806, they gave gifts to Clatsop chief Coboway as tokens of gratitude for his hospitality toward the foreign travelers.

Over the years, Mother Nature has wreaked havoc on the fort, and wet weather decayed much of the original wood. A reconstruction project was undertaken in 1955, and that replica lasted until October 2005 when it was destroyed by fire, just weeks before the site's bicentennial. The fort was replicated again the following year. The site is managed today by the National Park Service and offers a number of family-friendly activities, such as educational tours, guided trail walks, and canoe or kayak tours. The area boasts many scenic hiking opportunities, and an informative interpretive center has interactive exhibits that will keep children entertained.

As for the ghosts, don't be too surprised if you see any Native Americans or white men who look as if they belong to the early 1800s. They just might have roots to that very time when their mortal bodies stayed at the fort during a wet and dreary winter long ago. According to one rumor, the campgrounds are haunted by the ghost of a male figure dressed in military attire. He wanders the grounds at night, a rifle slung over his shoulder as if he's guarding those who sleep under his diligent watch.

Mystery of the Flavel House Museum

There are many wonderful things to see and experience in Astoria, a scenic oceanside community in northwest Oregon. This homey spot in the Pacific Northwest has several historic sites, some with tales of the supernatural and strange, but as with any place it is difficult to document them all. One of the more popular locations in Astoria with legends of ghosts is the Flavel House Museum.

Built in 1885 by wealthy businessman and riverboat pilot Capt. George Flavel, this spacious house is elegantly modeled in a Queen Anne Victorian style, featuring balconies, a hipped roof, and verandas. A three-story tower stands tall in the middle, while the inside of the 11,600-foot home is decorated with period furnishings and precious woodwork. The house, located at 441 8th Street, is said to have remained in the family until 1936 when Patricia Flavel, a great-granddaughter, donated it to Clatsop County. Today it is owned and operated by the Clatsop Historical Society, and the house and its carriage were listed on the National Register of Historic Places in 1980. Visitors can step back in time to Astoria's earlier days when touring the house, which you may do for a minimal price.

If you visit, keep an eye out for the paranormal, as it is rumored that there have been plenty of strange occurrences over the years. Old phones not plugged in mysteriously ring anyway, lights turn on and off by themselves, and window curtains open and close on their own. Are these disturbances caused by the spirit of Ol' Captain George or a member of his family? It is unknown, but believed likely. Members of Flavel's immediate family included his wife, Mary Boelling—who is rumored to have been only fourteen years old at the time of her marriage to thirty-year-old George—and their three children: Nellie, Katie, and George Conrad.

There's a second Flavel house in Astoria as well, but unlike this stately museum, the Harry Flavel house at 15th Street and Franklin Avenue is an abandoned and neglected building that looks as if it has its share of ghosts. This second home, built by George Conrad in 1901 several blocks from his parents' residence, eventually fell into the hands of his son, Harry M. Flavel. George, his wife, Florence, and their two children, Harry and Mary Louise, lived here until George passed away in 1951. After that, it was just the two children and their mother until, as the *Daily Astorian* puts it, "a mysterious day in 1990."

On that day, Mayor Willis Van Dusen, Community Development Director Brett Estes, building inspector Jack Applegate, and Astoria Police Chief Peter Curzon were able to gain access to the home, which had been the subject of local conversations for years. What they found was a house that, despite its outward appearance, was in fairly good shape despite its clutter of old newspapers, magazines, and other items the family hoarded.

"The family, once called the most prominent in Astoria, had dwindled down to a trio of recluses that disappeared into the night and will seemingly take their name with them when the last living member, Mary Louise Flavel, dies," reads the newspaper article.

And then, we can be sure, there'll be more talk of ghosts, perhaps at both Flavel homes.

The Restless Indian Spirit of Black Burial Canoe

Cemeteries and mausoleums are the obvious places to lay the deceased to rest, but there are countless other places that house the remains of the dearly departed. Hundreds of immigrants traveling the Oregon and Mormon Trails, for instance, were laid to rest on the lonely and lush prairies of America's Midwest and western landscapes. Thousands more, through misfortune, war, or disease, have made the ocean depths their grave. Many have been buried in lakes, reservoirs, and other places our minds might not even consider. For instance, have you ever thought of being buried in a boat? The casket of one Indian chief wound up being a canoe, which, if the tale is true, is haunted by the old Indian's restless spirit.

When Chief Comcomly died in 1830, according to an article by Lee Lewis Husk for *1859: Oregon's Magazine*, the chief's family placed his body in a raised war canoe in the family's burial grounds in Astoria to keep it from grave robbers. Later, a physician from the Hudson's Bay Company found the body and thought the dead chief's head would make a great "treasure." He decided it should be on display and removed it from the body.

"The head spent more than one hundred years in the Royal Naval Hospital Museum in Gosport, England," the article reads. "The chief's skull finally made its way back to Astoria, where the historical society displayed it as a curiosity in the Flavel House Museum for more than twenty years. In 1972, Chinook pleas for the return of the chief's skull were finally honored, and the chief was buried in an Ilwaco, Washington, graveyard north of his old village. Visitors can see the black burial canoe, now cast in concrete, that the city of Astoria built in 1961 as a memorial to the late Chief Comcomly."

Because the body was disrespected, some believe the old Indian chief has been restless ever since. His spirit supposedly haunts the site of the canoe memorial as a testament that he knows very well how his head and body were treated by the white man all those years ago.

The Monster with a Name

Over the years, countless renditions of aliens have been depicted on the silver screen and in books, many of them bald figures with big eyes that scarcely resemble human beings. And why should they? These movies and books are telling the stories of creatures beyond our reach and understanding.

Adding to the alien mystery are accounts of a creature that allegedly was very much like our modern Bigfoot, with a couple of exceptions. It had pointed catlike ears and shaggy white fur, thus perhaps resembling more the Abominable Snowman than Bigfoot. The beast, described as being around seven feet tall, once haunted Conser Lake and the surrounding area in Millersburg. It was called many things, including "The Conser Lake Monster," "The Ghost of Conser Lake," and even a "shaggy gorilla." These generic names offend the creature, however, reporter Betsy Westby explained in the now-defunct newspaper *Greater Oregon*. It's as if someone, instead of calling you by your name, says "Hey, you," or "that person."

According to one reporter and her psychic friend, this creature has a given name: Flix. The monster allegedly revealed his name telepathically to Westby and her psychic friend one morning in 1960 while the pair wandered through woods near Conser Lake. Interestingly, it was also during the 1960s that a flying saucer was said to have crashed into the lake. No saucer was ever found inside or outside the lake, but its furry white occupant was seen by many supposed witnesses, each describing it a little differently than the witness before, but with similar characteristics.

Flix, it seems, has made his appearance known to a number of people during the middle of the last century, including teenagers who'd visit the lake and surrounding area, sometimes playing jokes on each other in hopes of scaring their peers. Sightings began around 1959, after it was reported that a bright light had fallen into the lake. Rumors had it that an alien ship had crash-landed in Millersburg, and soon after sightings of a tall, furry white creature were reported in the woods near the lake.

Not unlike a daring dog, Flix (for lack of a better name for the strange monster) liked to chase vehicles. One truck driver, while driving in Millersburg, looked out his side window to see a furry white creature keeping pace with his vehicle. It wasn't the only encounter drivers had with the creature. One evening, a young couple driving near the lake also noticed a shaggy white figure keeping pace with their car. This behavior of running alongside cars is apparently a trait of Bigfoot-like creatures, for there've been several other reports of such creatures running alongside vehicles in different towns in Oregon, at least according to the blog Frame 352: The Stranger Side of Sasquatch.

If only aliens could talk, we would know from what realm the creature arrived. Strike that—Westby's friend supposedly had a telepathic conversation with the alien monster, who said it did not know from whence it came. What it did say was this: "I am not sure you could understand. It is hard to put it into earth terms." Then, hearing a party of hunters coming after him, it hurriedly ran away, never to be seen again. But before it departed, it left this imprint with Westby's psychic friend: "They are chasing me again. I mean no harm. Goodbye, friend. Come back. I am lonely."

Stories of the Ghost of Conser Lake—err, Flix—slowly quieted. Today, the lake is privately owned and not accessible to the general public. What does that mean for Flix? Is he still there, has he died, or has the Mother Ship come to take him back to his home beyond the stars?

Caught on Film: Oregon's Most Popular UFO Sighting

Every year, the people of McMinnville gather to celebrate the community's historic role in a UFO mystery. The annual McMenamins UFO Festival is touted as the second-largest alien festival in the country, having begun as a way to honor the legend that is known as the 1950 Trent Sighting.

On May 11, 1950, farmer Paul A. Trent and his wife went down in history as having captured on film one of the most notorious images of a UFO. Mrs. Trent was outside feeding her rabbits as the evening sun began to fade when something drew her attention to the sky—a large, disc-shaped object flying toward the family farm from the northeast. Not knowing what the object was, but believing it something her husband should see as well, she called to him. He joined her momentarily, then retreated back into the house for his camera. The object was still there when he returned, so Trent prepared his camera, found a place to shoot, and snapped the first picture. He rewound it and took a second shot, but that was all he could capture of the strange flying object in the sky before it vanished.

He did not get the film developed right away, but when he finally did the images of the UFO were there in plain sight. In one of the photos, the end of a shed or house can be seen on the left, and a telephone pole stands to the right, while the telephone wires help frame the top portion of the photograph. Below the wires in the background is a disc-shaped object that looks very much like the traditional UFO. The second picture is similar. In both snapshots, the UFO's top is leaning to the right, with its wider bottom part to the left.

It wasn't long before the images were on display at a local bank, but that was only the beginning of the fame that later would come to the Trents. A newspaper reporter saw the pictures and coaxed the couple into letting him publish an account of their story. They were reluctant at first, but soon relented, and the story was published in the local paper, the *McMinnville Telephone Register*. That caught the attention of *Life* magazine, which borrowed the negatives, and a story appeared in the national publication on June 26, 1950. Interestingly, the Trents did not receive back their famous photos for seventeen years because of the heavy investigation and analysis that went into the study.

What did those who analyzed the photographs think of them? There seemed to be no manipulation of the negatives, they concluded, saying the photographs seemed genuine. That, however, left the big question unanswered: What was captured on film on that otherwise uneventful evening in the late spring of 1950? By all accounts, it seemed as if the farmer couple had caught something extraordinary with their camera. Had they really experienced a close encounter of another kind?

Who's to say if aliens from outer space were driving the mysterious object? The Trents did seem to have captured something that was beyond their understanding and, likewise, beyond that of others as well. The photographs were studied by many eyes for more than a decade but no conclusive explanation was made as to what the images really are. The case, to this day, is filed as unexplained. Nevertheless, it is still celebrated. The McMenamins UFO Festival, held annually since 1999, is a fun family event that children and adults look forward to every year. Fans come dressed up in costume—some in full *Star Wars* regalia or space creations of their own making—while others come in their regular clothes but with minds just as fascinated by the possibility that there very well could be life beyond our known solar system.

Two Houses and Their Spirits

Two houses, several spirits—that about sums up the atmosphere of this next story of the McLoughlin and Barclay residences, historical homes in Oregon City. When I first heard their unusual story, I thought of the iconic 1950s television show *I Love Lucy*, which is just as funny today as when it aired. In the thirty-minute black-and-white sitcom, Lucy (a fireball redhead) and her Cuban Babalu–singing husband Ricky Ricardo lived in an apartment complex where their best friends also resided. What made the relationship a little awkward at times was that their friends, Fred and Ethel Mertz, were also the Ricardos' landlords. They'd show up at each other's doorsteps unannounced, inviting themselves in without ever knocking or ringing the doorbell. It didn't seem to bother either family.

Something similar, in a paranormal kind of way, happens at the McLoughlin and Barclay Houses, though when it does it usually does not strike the same humorous chord as television depictions. Ghosts are said to haunt both houses, their restless spirits wandering from one to the next, just as fast friends show up unannounced at each other's homes.

McLoughlin House

John McLoughlin, born in 1784 in Rivière-du-Loupe, Québec, Canada, was a shrewd businessman and superintendent of the British Hudson's Bay Company, but he was also a generous man who, against company orders, helped emigrants on the Oregon Trail garner supplies for the winter. (Officials feared white settlers would interfere with the lucrative fur trade in the area.) In hindsight, there might have been deeper meaning for his offerings of help. Contention between Great Britain and the United States was again reaching the boiling point, and McLoughlin assumed that, in the event of war, if he helped the traveling Americans they might think twice before attacking his outpost. Not all of the emigrants accepted his help, but those who did were grateful.

McLoughlin established Fort Vancouver on the Columbia River in 1825 and Oregon City in 1842. His name also lives on in the mansion-style home he built for his family in 1846. The good doctor would open it for visitors, including the emigrants whom he still helped, and for a time also served as the mayor of Oregon City.

Many were saddened at his passing on September 3, 1857. The home was sold and used for several things over the ensuing years, including a hotel, housing for Chinese laborers, apartment complex, and even a brothel. The elegant house that had once brought happiness to a compassionate man and his family was desecrated as a place for illicit sex, and yet it later would receive something of its former status thanks to those with a vision for its future.

According to the home's website, the house was threatened with demolition in 1909, but a concerned group of local citizens formed the McLoughlin Memorial Association "to preserve and protect the house and the legacy of Dr. McLoughlin. They moved the house from its original location by the river up to its present location atop the bluff, restored it, and turned the house into a museum." It was the first house in the West to be named by Congress as a national historic site, earning the designation in 1941. Sixty-two years later, in 2003, it was added to the National Park System as a unit of Fort Vancouver National Historic Site. It is deemed the oldest museum in the Beaver State.

Stories of ghosts at the McLoughlin House began sometime in the 1970s, after the bodies of McLoughlin and his wife, Marguerite, were moved from their original burial plot to a place between McLoughlin House and the neighboring Barclay House. Did this act serve as an invitation for their spirits to wander between the two homes, or is it a semblance of the nature of this friendly couple during their mortal lives?

Ghost stories associated with the McLoughlin House include the sighting of apparitions and phantom noises such as heavy footsteps on the stairs, harpsichord music playing in the dining room, and the sounds of a vacuum being operated upstairs. A rocking chair in the doctor's room supposedly moves of its own volition. It also is rumored that a certain picture inside the house glows every year on September 3, the day of Dr. McLoughlin's death, just as the sun rises to greet a new day. The spirit of Marguerite is believed to be the female-looking phantom seen at times gazing out the second-story window. And it is her phantom finger that allegedly taps the shoulders of unsuspecting housemaids as they go about their work, perhaps letting them know their work is observed by unseen eyes and that they might have missed a spot of dust. When the maids turn to see who is in the room with them, they see no one.

In paranormal circles, at least one room in the mansion is considered unfriendly: the parlor, where it is believed Mr. McLoughin passed from this life to the next. It has been rumored that a murder might have been committed in the same room long ago, but it is difficult to find anything concrete to support that story.

Evee Vann, a nearby resident, said she grew up hearing stories about the ghosts and has even seen strange shadow figures in the windows when the house was clearly closed to human occupancy. "I've definitely seen shadows in the windows at really odd hours," she said in a phone interview. "I don't know of anybody that grew up seeing the house that hasn't seen something strange there, shadows or faces in the windows. When I was about thirteen, I remember seeing what looked like a man and woman embracing in one of the windows. But there's no way anyone was in there. It's a historical site and it was locked up for the night."

Barclay House

Located in the same area, the Barclay House was built in 1849 by John L. Morrison as the home of Dr. Forbes Barclay. It is rumored to be haunted by the good doctor himself, who died in 1874. The house remained in the family until 1930, when it was moved from the waterfront to its present location next to the McLoughlin House. Today it contains museum offices and a gift shop.

Other spirits believed to roam the Barclay House include those of his brother, a woman, and a red-haired little boy with a faithful dog that follows him wherever he ventures. Most little boys are untidy, and it is believed this spirit is the one that leaves muddy footprints inside both mansions.

It's all conjecture, but perhaps the spirits of these former owners have become fast friends in the spirit world. According to lore, their shades have been seen, for whatever reason, inside both of the houses.

A Haunted History

There's an old building in Lincoln County that is haunted by its history. This shouldn't come as any surprise since the facility in question is the North Lincoln County Historical Museum at 4907 SW Highway 101. All hauntings in one form or another are tied to the history of an area. The history does not have to be tragic or terrorizing to make a place haunted. Life itself is full of energy and emotion, zest and enjoyment, so why can't hauntings thrive off that energy just as other, more malicious hauntings feed off negative energy? In any case, the ghosts rumored to haunt the historical museum are believed to be benevolent but busy spirits, sometimes attaching themselves to certain objects in the facility. Or maybe what people feel here are only remnants of the past.

"I have never seen an apparition, but I have felt things in the museum," said Anne Hall, the museum's executive director. "There seems to be, I feel, something associated with some of the objects when I handle them. I will get different feelings with different objects." She notices the vibes mostly when she moves objects to other locations in the building, such as when she places them in a new exhibit. "Strange things start to happen," she said. Hall will change an object's location only to find later that it has totally disappeared. She'll look for it high and low to no avail until later, as mysteriously as it disappeared, she will find it right back in its proper place.

One time, Hall said, a housemaid came to clean the bathroom. Upon entering the second time, she found a bathmat wet with soap and water. How could that happen? she wondered. She was in there just a few minutes before and everything was as it should be, with not a drop of water anywhere. No one else was inside the building at the time.

In some circles, there is a story about unseen beings once meeting in the conference room where their spirit bodies gathered around a table, discussing who knows what, but apparently something concerning the building and its venue as a benchmark to the past. These spirits, felt by psychics, likely were folks who during their mortal lives played a part in the county's history and the museum's mission. It is also said another spirit wanders the facility from room to room, letting its benevolent spirit be felt by those who sense its passing. Human voices have been heard inside the building when no one but a lone staffer was in the museum.

The museum was remodeled in 2004, Hall said, noting— perhaps ironically, since it often is said that paranormal activity increases during times of renovation—that unexplained activity has lessened since the remodel. But still, there are times when she feels not quite alone in the building even though she is the only mortal on the grounds at the time.

Visiting the museum is worth your time for the many things you'll learn about Lincoln County, and for the possible benevolent spirits you might sense here. Hall, who has worked for the museum since 2000, said she's not sure if the presences are actual spirits or the imprints their mortal frames left behind when they were alive.

"We perceive in our three-dimensional world maybe 1 percent or less of what's going on in the invisible world, but there's a lot of things going on we don't understand," Hall said "One thing is energy passing from one object to the next. There are objects here that were very personal to people who are no longer with us; I'm not sure if we're feeling their energy or a remnant of their presences."

A Janitor's Job is Never Done

Even spirits must have something to do, and for some people—and spirits—pushing a broom could be an enjoyable thing. Allegedly, a janitor who used to work at the Cheldelin Middle School in Corvalis died suddenly of a heart attack but still has fond attachments to his former job and place of work. Now, as a spirit entity, he supposedly still roams the school's hallways.

Lights turn on by themselves and the phantom sounds of a broom being pushed, happy whistling, and keys jangling have been heard in the building. The sounds always come from behind closed doors when no one is inside the rooms, but those who pass by on the outside will stop to listen. Sure as day, it sounds as if someone is doing the work of a janitor.

Could it be that the old janitor's spirit that haunts Cheldelin Middle School is just trying to relive happy moments from his past? The residual imprint perhaps comes to life when certain triggers occur in the school, whatever those might be.

The Ghosts of Chemawa

The spirits of former students are said to haunt their old stomping grounds, the Chemawa Indian School in Salem. The school, which started out serving elementary students in 1880 in Forest Grove, later moved to its current location in 1885 and has a long and interesting history. Opened on February 25, 1880, it was the brainchild of Richard Henry Pratt, who theorized that education was the best way to integrate Native Americans into general society. A series of schoolhouses soon opened, the first of which was the Carlisle Indian Industrial School near Harrisburg, Pennsylvania. The Chemawa Indian School was the second. Students came from Indian reservations in the area and were taught a variety of skills such as blacksmithing, carpentry, and shoemaking.

In 1884, a fire destroyed the girls' dormitory, just one of the factors that prompted officials to consider relocating the school. Several locations were considered, but officials chose the site five miles north of Salem because it was near the state capitol and served by a spur of the main railroad through the Willamette Valley. The school reopened as the Salem Indian Industrial and Training School on June 1, 1885, serving just half the students who attended the Forest Grove campus; the other half stayed in Forest Grove until additional buildings were completed at the new site. The school's first graduates completed their course of study the next year, having finished the sixth grade. Additional courses of study were added later, including agriculture training, and by 1900 the school had an enrollment of 453 students. Thirteen years later, 690 students were enrolled at the school. In 1922, the campus had seventy buildings, and enrollment peaked in 1926 at nearly 1,000 students. The following year it became a fully accredited high school, having dropped grades below six and added higher grade levels.

Eventually, enrollment dropped to around three hundred in the 1930s and the school was threatened with closure. It somehow survived and is still used today as a place of learning. In 2005 it partnered with Willamette University to provide tutoring several nights a week.

As with any building that's been around for as long as the Chemawa Indian School, stories of associated ghosts and the paranormal evolve. According to one popular story, there was a controversial death that allegedly happened at the school in 2003, when a female student died of alcohol poisoning after being locked in a cell while intoxicated. Could she be one of the spirits that supposedly haunts the old school campus?

There also might be older spirits involved with the hauntings, such as former Indian students who once attended here under government wishes to help them better integrate into a world new to the Indians. At the time the school was built, it was believed Indians were an inferior and uncivilized race. Education does help with integration and also helps clarify misconceptions. Thankfully, the American populace has been better educated since the early days of Chemawa and knows we're all human, just of different backgrounds and color. But do keep an eye out for those ghosts that supposedly still haunt the Chemawa campus. They might be from the "old school" ways of thinking.

Spirits at Oregon State University

Visit just about any college or university in the country and ask if there's been anything strange or paranormal associated with the campus. Chances are you'll hear something from someone about a dorm room, bathroom, bookshop, or auditorium that supposedly, whether through legend or actual witness experience, has a ghost attached to it. Schools of both higher and lower learning, for whatever reason—and there seem to be many—are some of the most haunted places.

Such is the case with Oregon State University. A female phantom is rumored to haunt Waldo Hall. Her apparition has been seen in the second-story hallway. She appears very much like a physical presence, but what catches people off guard is that when they glimpse her, she will slowly disappear into thin air. The spirit is believed to belong to Ida Kidder, the school's first librarian, who died in 1920. Kidder was, according to the lore, much loved by the students, who called her "Mother Kidder." With such affection placed upon her, it's no wonder her spirit might want to remain at the happy place she knew in mortality.

It's believed that other spirits haunt the former women's dormitory. Unnerving feelings suddenly come upon residents, as if unseen presences are near, and doors have been known to slam on their own.

A second female spirit lurks in another room on campus. The spirit, according to the story, belongs to a student who was killed in that very room in Sackett Hall during the 1950s. Still angry about the senseless crime committed against her, the female's spirit lashes out, throwing objects around the room and starting fires for which no logical explanation could account.

Do ghosts really get angry? Yes, and according to some paranormal researchers, there are several different reasons why a spirit might be malevolent. The first, of course, is that the entity itself is an evil spirit, perhaps something demonic. Other spirits might feel they were wronged in mortality and have some sort of hostility that they just can't seem to shake except through aggressive hauntings. Some spirits might try to scare the hell out of a person to get his or her attention, like a good Hollywood movie depicts, in an effort to teach someone about the spirit's mortal passing. Another theory is that spirits of suicide victims might be scared to cross over because they're afraid of the judgment awaiting them on the other side.

The Pacific Paranormal Research Society states: "Ghosts have traditionally been seen as spirits looking for revenge, or people who have died a violent or gruesome death. Although this may be true in some cases, the true description of a ghost is someone who has decided, for whatever reason, to stay behind and not go to where they are supposed to. Most do so out of choice, although some individuals may not realize that they have actually died. Ghosts can be conscious or unconscious."

In light of these theories, it appears that this spirit of Oregon State University is angry at her early, unjustified demise. Her presence has sometimes been reported as a swirling mist, perhaps as another demonstration of her anger at being taken from mortality before her time.

The Werewolf of Estacada

Werewolves, vampires, and ghouls, oh my! If you think such things were only in fiction or made up in horror novels and movies, think again. At least, that's what some people say who claim to have seen actual werewolves stalk the dark nights of Oregon.

Sightings of werewolves—fantastical creatures that are half man, half beast—are not as uncommon as you might think. There have been numerous reports of such alleged sightings in many parts of the country, perhaps the most famous being the Beast of Bray Road in Elkhorn, Wisconsin. According to author and newspaper reporter Linda Godfrey in her book *Monsters of Wisconsin*, witnesses described the hairy creature as resembling a bear, wolf, and even a Bigfoot. The wolf description is the most popular, mainly because the beast was seen walking on all four legs, much like a dog, instead of the usual Bigfoot sightings of a tall, bipedal creature. If there really are such things as werewolf-like creatures that exist in the country's Midwest, then who's to say there cannot also be such creatures in the Pacific Northwest? Like Bigfoot, if such creatures truly exist, they likely get around, reproducing and evolving.

According to one website entry, a newspaper carrier from Estacada, Oregon, saw such a creature while in his car delivering papers early one morning. He had to quickly press his brakes when a large doglike creature ran in front of him. Thinking it was nothing more than a loose canine, he changed his mind when he got a better look at the beast. He described it as having large hind legs but small front legs. The one thing about his description that differed from others was that the beast appeared to be hairless, with pink skin. The creature continued to run until it abruptly sat down in the middle of the road. Then, just as quickly, it ran into the woods from whence it had come. This was the first and only sighting by the witness, but he claims he had heard of other similar reports in the area.

Does it mean that what he saw was a werewolf or something else out of science fiction and the weird? No, of course not—it could indeed have been a strange breed of dog or other animal. But then again, in our world of mysteries and ghosts, who's to say it was not something more sinister? One good thing is that the creature, whatever it was, did not act like a Hollywood rendition of a werewolf. If it had, it likely would have attacked the man's car and torn the unsuspecting driver to shreds.

The next time you're on a dark road in Estacada, or anywhere else in the Beaver State, keep an out for this modern, hairless werewolf of northwest Oregon.

The Ghosts of Cannon Beach

Those who visit Cannon Beach in Clatsop County will most likely remember two things. The first is the mysterious sand that glows blue-green because of an infestation of phytoplankton. These microscopic creatures emit a glowing energy when touched or moved.

The second is the popular 235-foot Haystack Rock in the beach's southwest corner near Tolovana Park. The rock, which has a small cave system and often is accessible at low tide, shares the beach with two siblings called the Needles—two tall rocks that stand erect in the water like giant thumbs pointing out of the ocean. These rocks help define Cannon Beach, making it an iconic place to visit along the Oregon coast.

While the beach is a postcard setting, there's allegedly something more ominous about it as well. It is defined, according to lore, not only by the tall rocks but also by tall stories of ghosts and mummies that roam the sandy crest in this otherwise harmonious site.

The Argonutua Beach House allegedly is haunted by the spirit of a man named Ghengis Hansel, who mysteriously disappeared while staying at the house in 1952 and was never seen again, at least not as a mortal. As the legend goes, some people who stayed in the beach house claimed to have encountered the ghost of Hansel, while others say they have sensed a disquieting presence in the house, which supposedly has many secret doors and compartments. Did Hansel, while still alive, become trapped in one of those secret chambers? Or are these hidden passageways the fodder that sparked the ghost tale?

No stories about bodies being found within the compartments have arisen, at least not that I could find. Perhaps then, the only way to find out if it truly is haunted is by visiting yourself. While there, ask the staff if they've had any encounters with ol' Hansel.

You can also see what staff will tell you about the phantom mummy, named Bandage Man, that supposedly haunts the short approach from Highway 101.

Bandage Man, according to the story, is believed to be the spirit of a die-hard criminal who escaped prison in the early or mid-1900s and was never found by police. The bandages he wears come from the dressings he received after being shot multiple times by police before his arrest. Somehow he survived, according to legend, and after time at a hospital he was transferred to jail, still wrapped in his bandages. On the way, he escaped and fled into the woods. Since his escape, he has been accused of murdering several people and animals. In more recent years, a mummy-like figure has attacked people on the short route, leaving pieces of his bandages behind.

Are these tall tales or something more real? Perhaps only those who encounter these supernatural beings will ever know. Real or not, these stories help define Cannon Beach as a very mysterious place to visit.

The Warlock of Mason's Cemetery

Some legends die hard, while others slowly fade into oblivion. Those that remain do so for at least two reasons: they either come very close to the truth, or they're such interesting stories that they continue to be passed around, sometimes embellished and added upon but surviving nonetheless.

I think the story of Mason's Cemetery in Corvallis, where a warlock, or male witch, supposedly was buried in the cemetery's early days, is an example of an embellished tale. As the story goes, the man was not only a warlock but also a gigolo to boot, seducing a number of the town's married women. We're not sure how he died, but it could have been revenge by the women's irate husbands.

Nonetheless, his icy personality has been felt even after his demise, for it is said that if you go to the cemetery at a certain spot, the warlock's spirit will appear next to you. You'll know you're in the right spot—and that he's nearby—not so much by seeing an apparition but by feeling a cool breeze upon your skin.

The Legends of Yaquina Bay Lighthouse

Lightning flashed in the darkened sky. Seconds later, thunder boomed overhead. The teenagers ran faster, hoping to reach shelter before they were drenched by the rain that spattered the sandy ground about them. Electricity streaked the night sky once more, lighting their path. Almost there—and then at last they were inside the Yaquina Bay Lighthouse. Later, once the storm had passed, all of the teens came out of the lighthouse.

All of them, that is, except one. The spirit of a young woman, according to the legend, haunts the lighthouse to this day. It is unknown how she met her demise because her body was never found, and her disappearance is still a mystery. When police arrived, all they found was the young woman's bloody handkerchief at the bottom of the third-floor staircase. Or so the story goes.

The lighthouse was built in 1871 in Newport but only operated for three years before it was decommissioned and replaced by the more modern Yaquina Head Lighthouse, located three miles north of the bay. Over the next century, the original lighthouse fell into disrepair, and out of its seclusion grew the ghost stories and urban legends. "It stands upon a promontory that juts out dividing the bay from the ocean, and is exposed to every wind that blows. Its weather-beaten walls are wrapped in mystery," reads a description in the November 1899 edition of *Pacific Monthly*. "Of an afternoon when the fog comes drifting in from the sea and completely envelopes the lighthouse, and then stops in its course as if its object had been attained, it is the loneliest place in the world. At such times those who chance to be in the vicinity hear a moaning sound like the cry of one in pain, and sometimes a frenzied call for help pierces the death-like stillness of the waning day. Far out at sea, ships passing in the night are often guided in their course by a light that gleams from the lantern tower where no lamp is ever trimmed."

While the teenage woman's body was never found, her spirit— or at least signs of its alleged presence appearing in the form of eerie lights in the upstairs window—has since been seen on occasion in the lighthouse.

Some people, including a state parks department official, say the story about the teenagers is fiction and that there's a logical explanation for the strange lights people claim to witness. One theory is light escaping from the beacon above. Others claim to have seen no lights at all, but say they've heard crying and moaning from deep inside the lighthouse. Skeptics look to the wind for an earthly explanation of such sounds, but how does that resolve the issue when no wind reaches inside to where the moaning cries originate?

It very well could be that the story about the teenagers who ventured to the lighthouse on a dark and stormy night more than a century ago is nothing more than urban legend. But folklore and legend often begin with kernels of truth. What's the truth behind the Yaquina Bay Lighthouse?

There's another similar story associated with the lighthouse that involves mutiny and a captain's ghost. According to this legend, in 1874 the crew of the whaling ship *Monkton* mutinied against Capt. Evan McClure and set him adrift in a small lifeboat. It was the last time anyone saw the red-haired captain alive, but later on people who knew him in life claimed to see his spirit in homes and taverns along the coast. One description that has been handed down of the ghostly figure says that his face, when seen, resembles that of a skeleton.

People began to wonder why the restless captain's spirit haunted their homes and businesses instead of those of his crew that set him adrift. Was he only looking for a place to rest? If so, he apparently found it in the Yaquina Bay Lighthouse, abandoned that same year.

One day after Captain McClure's ghost took up residence at the lighthouse, a young girl and her friends were picnicking in what is today's Yaquina Bay State Park. The girl entered the lighthouse to retrieve a scarf she had left there earlier and then gave a deathly scream. Her friends, who had remained outside, heard the terror in her voice and the door slam shut. Like with the captain when he was set adrift, it was the last time anyone saw the young girl alive. No one knows what happened to her, but her spirit, according to the legend, has joined the restless captain and the other female presence in the lighthouse. They have been seen there for more than a hundred years—McClure with his captain's hat and skeletal face, and the girl in a flowing white dress with her scarf.

Thrill-Seeking Bigfoots and Sasquatches

On countless highways across the United States, hundreds or perhaps thousands of animals reach their journey's end by being run over by cars and trucks. Killed on America's roadways, we know the dead animals as "roadkill," an aim at lightheartedness in the face of a rather serious and tragic epidemic: too many animals shuttered on America's roadways and byways.

I can't help but wonder what The RoadKill Café would call a Bigfoot or Sasquatch, if one ever were to be hit and killed on the highway. Such a creature apparently came close to becoming roadkill after a family from Idaho almost hit one near Multnomah Falls, Oregon, in the early part of this century.

Linda Boydson and her son were driving through the area one night when they encountered the nine-foot-tall hairy man. Unlike other Bigfoots sighted and described as large in stature, this one seemed as if it hadn't had a meal in quite a while. It was thin, comparatively speaking, Linda was reported as saying on the Bigfoot Encounters website. Apparently the creature was standing in the slow lane when Boydson and her son came upon the beast. "She barely missed hitting the creature—probably because it was so skinny," the report reads.

This stirs a question: What do Bigfoots eat? Are they vegetarian or do they like a little meat once in a while? I can't recall hearing or reading of one being seen eating, though there have been incidences of fresh meat or other foodstuff missing from lonely homes and campsites where Sasquatch has been rumored to haunt. Like Bigfoot, it all is conjuncture and speculation until we know more. And that, I'd say, would have been the only positive thing to come of it if Boydson had actually hit the hairy man. We would have had an actual Sasquatch body to study—unless government officials came to whisk the creature away. In any case, I came up with a roadkill name for Sasquatch: "Flatfooted Bigfoot."

Another Sasquatch legend in Oregon involves a Bigfoot that allegedly disguises itself as the famous fire marshal Smokey Bear. According to a story on OregonBigfoot.com, a group of friends was camping in February 2002 near the top of Goat Mountain in the forests near Clackamas when they encountered a beastly creature that didn't seem to appreciate the campfire the friends had started.

While the friends chatted at their camp, they suddenly heard noises all around them, as if something large were walking through the brush. When they shined their flashlights into the darkness of the trees, the noises would stop. When they moved the flashlights away from the trees, the noises would begin again.

During one of these intervals, while the lights were fixed on the darkness beyond, they heard another noise. They turned their lights in the direction of the new sound and saw a large tree falling. It landed right on top of their campfire. In the rim of the lights, they saw a hairy, manlike creature stalking off into the darkness, breaking branches off more trees as it hastily departed.

The Witch of Lafayette Cemetery

The stereotypical description of a witch might read something like this: an ugly, older woman with a crooked nose who wears a black hat and gown, and perhaps holds a broom or stirs a cauldron. Such a depiction does justice to cartoons and Disney movies, but it's not a correct representation of real-life witches. They do not fly around on broomsticks, for instance, but they might cast a spell or two.

Yes, there are such things as witches. The Bible, Christendom's most holy book, attests to the reality of witches and the power they may wield, though most are pacifists and unassuming.

A witch, in one sense, is someone who practices the black arts or evil magic—in other words, witchcraft. Another modern definition is "a practitioner of Wicca." Though some say Wicca—also known as the "witch-cult" religion—originated in the sixteenth and seventeenth centuries, the modern movement became popular in the 1950s in Britain courtesy of one of its main proponents, Gerald Gardner, one of the first Wiccans to publicly share his beliefs. The religion soon spread to other English-speaking countries, including the United States, where it was further modified by new supporters who formed their own covens but kept the same system of beliefs. Most practitioners of modern Wicca are peaceful, pantheistic and polytheistic, and believe in the importance of feminine principles and respect for nature, but this does little to lessen their image in the eyes of those who believe that Wicca is associated with the black arts.

One ornery witch of the more blatant kind, according to local lore, supposedly haunts Lafayette Cemetery. According to the story, the witch—no one is quite sure of her name—was hanged for witchcraft long ago and then buried in the cemetery. Her restless spirit has been seen by late-night cemetery visitors, some of whom say they've been chased by the evil entity. Others say they've heard the witch's cackle or seen her apparition walk among the grave markers. What's more unnerving is the witch's prediction, which is one event away from being fulfilled.

While she stood before her accusers, a rope around her neck before the fateful drop that would bring her death, the woman cursed the people and their town of Lafayette, saying it would burn to the ground three times. Every time they'd rebuild, flames would again destroy it. So far, fire has destroyed portions of the town twice.

Lafayette, located between McMinnville and Dundee in Yamhill County, was incorporated by the Oregon Legislative Assembly on October 17, 1878, and in 2010 had a population of 3,742. It was founded in 1847 by Joel Perkins, an early pioneer to Oregon Territory. The town grew quickly after the discovery of gold in

California, and by the 1850s it had become one of the richest cities in Oregon. Let's hope the witch's prediction is just fairytale and that a third fire won't harm the town or its peaceful residents.

Guardian Pirate Spirits of a Lost Treasure

Everyone likes an adventure story. One of my favorite modern-day adventure writers is Clive Cussler, whose high-paced yarns take place on land and sea—and sometimes even under the sea. Several of his books involve searches for lost treasure. And who can forget that classic book *Treasure Island* by Robert Louis Stevenson? It is one of my son's favorite childhood books.

What is it about adventure stories, especially when they deal with the search for lost treasure, that captivates the mind? I think it is the allure of experiencing adventure, visiting distant lands, and finding something lost through the printed page that we in the real world will never do. That's why I was excited when I came across the following story about seedy pirates, their flag-furled ships, and chests of gold, diamonds, and pearls.

The time period is the 1700s and the setting is just off the coast near present-day Tillamook. Two ships, their sails unfurled, stare each other down, firing their cannons. One of them is successful, sending its opponent to the shores near Neahkahnie Mountain. Once marooned, the ship's crew leaves the vessel, taking with them one item that was particularly valuable: a treasure chest filled with their dreams' worth of riches. Fearing for their lives, but fearing for the treasure's safety more, the crew digs a hole in the sand and buries the chest. If their enemies were to come ashore to give battle, at least the treasure would stay out of their hands.

Their opponents might not have seen the crew's desperate act to save the treasure, but other hidden eyes saw what they did with the valuables. Indians hiding in the nearby brush witnessed the burial of the treasure chest. Many of the pirates apparently survived the battle (if there really was one at all) because they later befriended the coast's native inhabitants. The Indians, however, didn't reciprocate in kind. One night while the sailors slept, a band of Tillamook Indians sneaked into camp and slaughtered the white men in their beds. They then took the bloodied bodies and buried them near the hidden treasure. Why they did this, or why they did not unearth the treasure chest for themselves, is unknown, but it apparently has served at least one purpose. It is said that the spirits of the dead pirates still watch over their buried treasure.

Many have come here, some with metal detectors, in an effort to locate the treasure, but it remains lost to this day, though the spirits will manifest themselves if you get too close to finding where it is located. For some, the search has proven deadly—over the years, several who have tried looking for it have died accidental deaths in their attempts to find it.

The Indian Maiden Who Gave Her Life for Her People

Stories abound in folklore and legend about Indian maidens who, for one reason or another, give up their lives either for a cause or because of a broken heart. The latter often has the maiden jumping off a mountain peak, either because her fiancé died in battle or because of the conflict between differing tribes and being unable to marry her young brave. In such a state, imagining her life without her true love, the maiden decides the best thing is to put an end to her life. Ever after, her spirit is said to haunt the place of her demise.

In this story, however, the young Indian girl who gave up her life did so for a completely selfless reason: to save her tribe from imminent death. As the legend has it, a medicine man told the girl that if her people were to be saved from an epidemic then raging among the tribes, a sacrifice would have to be made to appease the gods and prevent the further spread of the illness. The young virgin girl, considering the welfare of her people against her own, offered herself. Accordingly, she climbed the 542-foot-tall Upper Multnomah Falls, located east of present-day Troutdale between Corbett and Dodson, and flung herself to a sacrificial end. It worked, according to the legend, because the disease abated. The maiden's spirit, however, continues to haunt this allegedly sacred ground.

Visiting the falls, touted by the U.S. Forest Service as the second-tallest year-round waterfall in the country, is a pleasure because of the serene beauty and misty atmosphere. Water here free falls for more than five hundred feet into a pool before falling a second time, for a shorter distance, under an arching stone footbridge built in 1914. If you see the spirit of an Indian maiden, give her a nod, because it's probably the same one who saved her people from ill health and calamity.

Ghosts of the Rock Piles

There's something to be said for small towns. They're usually quiet places to live, there's not a lot of traffic, and oftentimes neighborly kindness runs rampant because residents know each other. When a stranger comes to town, he or she might stick out like a sore thumb, but that won't stop the townsfolk from gathering the welcoming committee. But what if the visitor is a specter from the Great Beyond? Do you welcome it, too, and if so, how?

The ghosts that show up at a place locally known as the Rock Piles near Idanha, a roughly two-square-mile town on the Marion and Linn Counties border, don't stick around long enough to either be welcomed or shunned. They appear seemingly out of nowhere and just as suddenly disappear.

According to local lore, the spectral images seen here have been those of a headless logger, a skinless dog, and a little girl donning a white dress. There's even a rumor that the apparition of a woman has been seen hanging from a tree with a noose around her neck.

Why such images? Why so many ghosts? Do the stories have basis in fact, or are they made up to be passed around in schools and paranormal circles? When it comes to the paranormal—a subject that is fun to read and talk about but difficult to come to any conclusive evidence for—conjecture is sometimes half the tale. One thing is for sure, though, if the story is true: For such a small town—according to census records, Idanha had just 136 residents in 2012—it sure has its fair share of ghosts.

Central Coast
and Southwest Corner

SCENIC BEACHES, OLD LIGHTHOUSES, NEIGHBORLY COMMUNITIES, AND plenty of history and hauntings make up Oregon's central coast and southwest corner. In this section, which covers areas in Lane, Coos, Curry, Douglas, Josephine, Jackson, and Klamath Counties, you'll read about Rue, the Lady in Gray who haunts an old lighthouse in search for her long-lost daughter; strange encounters with Bigfoot; one of the Beaver State's most famous and puzzling locations, the weird and wacky Oregon Vortex; and another woman's spirit who, although kind to guests, roams an iconic chateau. There's more, of course, so read on and be unnerved.

Legend of the Lady in Gray

More than a century ago, a young girl drowned in the estuary near Florence. But it is not her spirit that reportedly haunts the Heceta Head Lighthouse. That honor goes to the girl's mother, the wife of an assistant lightkeeper. After the loss of her daughter, she was so distraught that she no longer found value in living and ended her own life.

The location of the girl's grave is unknown, though a headstone supposedly resides somewhere in the vegetation surrounding the

lighthouse. The restless spirit of her mother has been reported on numerous occasions at or near the lighthouse, supposedly searching for her lost daughter. Donning a gray dress, fitting for her melancholy state, the spirit has been named by her many witnesses as the "Lady in Gray," or simply as "Rue."

One story of her appearance comes from the 1970s, when a worker cleaning windows came face-to-face with the ghost and fled in terror. So frightened was the man that he said he would only return to work if he didn't have to visit the attic, which apparently is where he saw the ghostly shade. At one point, he broke an attic window from the outside of the building, but refused to go inside to clean it up. That very night, a couple who lived there at the time reported hearing scraping sounds upstairs. After going up to investigate, they found small shards of glass all swept up and placed in a neat little pile in the corner of the room. Rumor has it that Rue, a tidy spirit, had cleaned up the worker's mess.

The fifty-six-foot-tall lighthouse, built in 1893 thirteen miles north of Florence, is named after Spanish explorer Bruno de Heceta, who explored the Pacific Northwest in the late 1700s. With a beam that's visible for more than twenty-one miles, it is one the strongest lights along the Oregon Coast. The light today is maintained by the Oregon Parks and Recreation Department. The assistant lightkeeper's house, operated as a bed-and-breakfast, is maintained by the U.S. Forest Service.

Visitors come to enjoy the salt breezes and ocean view at the historic landmark. While here, they usually hear a tale or two of the Lady in Gray, as stories about her are as much a part of the lighthouse as its iconic location among the scenic cliff line. Every once in a while, to confirm that the stories just might be true, a patron walks away from the lighthouse claiming to have had a personal encounter with the friendly, albeit sad ghost lady.

Such stories are not tied to folklore and legend only. Once, while at a book signing in Utah, I met a woman who said she visited the lighthouse as a little girl. To this day, she remembers what she saw upon looking in one of its windows: the image of a gray lady rocking in a chair.

The Wacky and Weird Oregon Vortex

Feeling a little overweight lately? Or maybe you'd like to put on a few pounds. To make yourself feel better, try visiting the Oregon Vortex in Gold Hill, one of the Beaver State's wackiest and weirdest places. Here, brooms stand upright by themselves; round objects roll uphill; and, depending on which direction you walk at certain places at the site, you will appear to either grow tall and skinny or short and round.

"The Oregon Vortex is a glimpse of a strange world where the improbable is the commonplace and everyday physical facts are reversed," reads a description on the location's website. "It is an area of naturally occurring visual and perceptual phenomena, which can be captured on film." That's good, because it's difficult to describe in words what this place really is and how the visual effects work.

The same website describes the site as naturally inclined to strange phenomena long before the current attraction's facilities were built. A vortex, according to Merriam-Webster, is "something that resembles a whirlpool," or "a mass of fluid (as liquid) with a whirling or circular motion that tends to form a cavity or vacuum in the center of the circle and to draw toward this cavity or vacuum bodies subject to its action." While the Oregon Vortex is anything but liquid, the same type of action seems to happen here in a mystic, almost paranormal way—there's a type of cavity or vacuum in which strange things happen. The website describes it as a spherical force field, with half above ground and half below.

The Old Grey Eagle Mining Company built a small shed on the property in 1904, using it as a storage facility and assay office. The shed is known today as The House of Mystery, a slanted, eerie-looking structure that is a premier tourist spot. The Oregon Vortex was founded as a modern-day attraction by John Litser, who opened it to the public in the 1930s. Litser, a geologist and physicist, started studying the area the previous decade and performed a number of experiments at the site, trying to find out what physical properties made it seem like a vortex for the unexplained. Apparently, the area was already considered forbidden by Native Americans, who claimed that things they could not explain occurred here. Their horses refused to enter the "vortex," and young braves would surrender their title when near what they considered to be the unholy ground.

Legend tells that after compiling his findings, Lister burned his notes because, he allegedly said, "The world is not ready for this." He continued to study the vortex until his death in 1959, believing that something paranormal existed here.

Skeptics say the strange effects—such as the apparent height change of two people, depending on where they stand—are nothing more than optical illusions, like a distorted background, for instance, which creates a "forced perspective." But what perspective is it when witnessing an apparition? According to some, the ghost of John Litster has been seen in the area, most often at the House of Mystery. His spirit appears very much like an older gentleman dressed in period clothing, often with a big smile on his face as he watches visitors crack smiles of their own as they experience the Oregon Vortex.

Visit the attraction's website, which, through its descriptions and photographs, tells of the strange phenomena that occur here. And then, if you haven't done so already, make a plan to visit this weird and wacky place that will put you face-to-face with one of Oregon's most bizarre phenomena.

Mysterious Creatures of Crater Lake

Nearly eight thousand years ago, a volcanic mountain located in present-day south-central Oregon collapsed after erupting in a giant burst that sent magma and ash twelve thousand feet into the air. The eruption thrust debris across the West and into Canada. As the magma, which reached three miles below the mountain's surface, fed the eruption and the inner chambers collapsed, the destructive force formed a bowl, or caldera. This crater later filled with water.

In essence, Mother Nature turned the very mountain peak, once called Mount Mazama, into one of Oregon's most famous lakes. You know it as Crater Lake, a twenty-square-mile body of water located in the Cascade Range at Crater Lake National Park. As with most movement in nature, evolution and nature's miracles don't happen overnight. It is estimated that it took around two hundred and fifty years of rain and snow to fill the caldera to its present water level.

Viewing the lake aerially, it looks as if a meteor crash-landed into the mountain, creating the giant crater that today is a popular place for fishing, hiking, and photography. In lore, however, the lake and surrounding wilderness are haunted by ghosts, Bigfoot, UFOs, and lake monsters. Why this scenic and tranquil spot in Oregon Country attracts the paranormal and strange is unclear, but it apparently has done so for decades, serving as some sort of conduit for such activity since before the arrival of the white man.

Rumor has it that some visitors to the area have disappeared, never to be seen or heard from again. That, according to the stories, was the very thing the Klamath Indians feared most about the area. It was not a happy place, they said. Another tribe, the Modoc Indians, described it as the home of dark spirits.

There's another story to the lake, this one coming from the Klamath. As legend has it, they believe that the Great Spirit collapsed the mountain on a band of rebelling braves. Afterward, according to an article by Cody Meyocks on the blog Who Forted?, "the Great Spirit converted the ghosts of the victims into huge, long-armed dragons which could reach up to the crater's rim and drag down any venturesome warrior. These kidnapping 'dragons' have also been described as 'giant crayfish' in Klamath lore. Similar ghouls have been spotted even in modern times." The Klamath version of the devil also is said to live in the lake, according to another Indian legend.

More modern stories tell of strange lights seen in the skies overhead; hairy, manlike creatures that stalk the woods; phantom figures that dart about; and large water creatures, described as monsters, that inhabit the chilly depths of the iconic lake. It is told that two Sasquatch were killed in the area—one by car and the other by train. The first was allegedly taken away by government agents, and the other was never officially reported.

That alone brings up the topic of government cover-ups and the reality of Bigfoot. If the story is true about government agents whisking away a fallen Sasquatch, what did they do with the creature? Why has there not been any published, documented proof that such creatures truly exist? Why hasn't the deceased beast been placed in a museum?

Some questions might be better left unanswered anyway, such as the mystery that surrounds Crater Lake. If we knew all the whys of the area's strange phenomena, perhaps we'd be inclined to stay clear of it. In part, it's the mystery that keeps the intrigue of the lake alive and keeps us coming back again and again.

As for the lake's future, will it forever remain as it is now? Will the mountain one day erupt again? There is always that possibility, according to those who've studied the geology of the mountain. Studies indicate that water enters the lake from the bottom, where it is heated by hot rock beneath the fractured caldera floor. It's uncertain if magma still resides in the dark abyss, but don't put it past the mountain to blow its top again, lake or not, and water monster or no monster. After all, Mother Nature herself is sometimes a beast.

Shakespearean Ghosts

The famous poet and playwright William Shakespeare made a name for himself that has survived for more than four hundred years. Shakespeare was born on April 23, 1564, in Stratford-upon-Avon and lived to the ripe young age of forty-nine, passing away on April 23, 1616. His many plays and poems have lived on not only in book form but also on the world's stages where they rightly belong.

One such venue is the Oregon Shakespearean Festival Theater at 15 S. Pioneer Street in Ashland, Jackson County. The theater was founded by Angus L. Bowmer, a young teacher from Southern Oregon Normal School (now Southern Oregon University), who, according to the group's website, "was struck by the resemblance between the Chautauqua walls and some sketches he had seen of Elizabethan theatres."

He proposed producing a "festival" of two plays. The city provided him with means to do so, and the stage was built. On July 2, 1935, it came to life with the production of *Twelfth Night*, followed soon thereafter with *The Merchant of Venice*. Times have changed since then, when reserved seats cost merely $1 and general admission was 50 cents (children were admitted for 25 cents), but the enjoyment of the plays has remained. And there's a little something else of the past that, according to the stories, has remained on stage with the human actors: benevolent spirits.

In 1946, during the performance of *King Lear*, it is said that the ghost of English actor and director Charles Laughton appeared on stage, fulfilling his wish to play the part at the Ashland Theater. He passed away before he could perform the role in his mortal life, but it looks as if he came back to take part in it as a spiritual being.

Another spirit, this one of a tall male figure, is said to sing madrigals on the third floor of the Elizabethan Playhouse. No one is sure to whom this spirit belongs, but it's likely he had ties to the place while alive, probably as a former actor and singer. If not, then we can only assume it is the spirit of someone who used to visit the playhouse or some mysterious fan of the old Bard.

The Chetco Indian Devil

The little girl is tucked into bed, a little fearful about the thing she knows lives in her closest and comes out to scare her at night just as she dozes off to the land of Nod. Slowly, the closet door opens. Nothing but blackness is seen inside, until the eyes appear. And then a hand emerges from behind the door and—Boo!—a monster makes his appearance, frightening the young child, who screams at the top of her lungs.

Sound familiar? You've probably seen something similar in the Pixar-animated movie *Monsters Inc.*, one of the children's films I enjoy watching. The movie is creative, funny, and ironic. In the film, "real-life monsters" work eight-hour jobs learning and putting into practice the art of scaring young children. The parents, of course, think their children are letting their imaginations get the best of them, but the kids know better. So do those who've encountered the Chetco Indian Devil, also known as "The Wild Man" or "Sasquatch," but most popularly called Bigfoot.

Or at least, that's what we assume the creature was that supposedly roamed the countryside near Myrtle Point in the early 1900s. The physical apparition of the creature is rumored to have haunted workers of the Sixes Mining Company. Many described the alleged "monster" as an upright, two-legged creature covered in coarse-looking hair. They'd hear it walking outside their cabins, see it in the woods, and smell its foul stench in the otherwise clean mountain air. One time, according to a report, it grabbed hold of the corner of a cabin and shook the structure, all the while making a strange whistling sound.

That'd be enough to frighten children in their beds, movie or not, and it apparently also frightened the adult workers. One man allegedly took aim at the creature with his rifle, but when he pulled the trigger he missed, scaring the creature into the woods. It didn't stay away for long, however, because more sightings of the beast occurred. No one could quite make out what the creature was, and so the names began. The Chetco Indian Devil name comes from a description of the creature as standing around seven feet tall, smart enough to throw rocks with accuracy, and very much resembling the devil—ill-tempered and ornery, with a sort of childlike mischievousness about him, just like those silly monsters in the movie.

Haunts at the Herman Helms House

For some unlucky souls, even death isn't an escape from trial and misfortune. The sorrow felt in this life seems to linger for at least a couple of spirits who, rumor has it, haunt the Herman Helms House in Jacksonville. Interestingly, neither of them is believed to be the spirit of Herman himself.

One of the spirits is that of an elderly woman, Herman's wife August, who roams the building, her pitiful sobs heard throughout the house. The other spirit is that of a young girl, believed to be their daughter Herminne Helms, who died in 1868 of smallpox. She is sometimes seen at the bottom of the stairs, also crying.

The reason for their sorrow is evident if you know a little about the Helms family, who in the mid- to late 1800s lost several family members to disease, murder, and suicide. This type of haunting is one that demonstrates the powerful link that binds families and their concern for each other.

In religious terms, August and Herminne have long since reunited in the spirit world, after their deaths. Herminne no longer suffers from illness and disease, and all of the Helms family members are in some way together again. So then why the sorrow from August and Herminne, demonstrated as hauntings since their own mortal bodies have passed from this life?

This simply is a residual haunting of their past sorrows, which left such an imprint in the space-time continuum that they have repeated themselves to unsuspecting modern-day witnesses. Such is the impact of life, love, death, and family relationships. Perhaps there's a moral lesson taught here, too: The notion of ghosts suggests that there is life after death and that we don't stop caring for people, especially those closest to our hearts, when we pass from this life into the next. What happens to them is very much a concern, which can fill us with peace, worry, or despair.

Like mother, like daughter. Both of them experienced tragedy during their mortal lives, and now as spirits they still experience the worry and sadness that have enveloped them for more than a hundred years. It has been said that time heals all wounds. Will it ever heal those of these two still-sad spirits?

Ghost Woman of the Chateau

It was supposed to be a day to remember for young Elizabeth, the best day of her life. She had met the man of her dreams, fell in love, and finally was married. The couple picked a place to spend their honeymoon—the Chateau at Oregon Caves, a rustic but beautiful six-story hotel built in 1934 that sits over a stream between two steep glades in the Oregon wilderness in the Siskiyou Mountains.

Being in such a beautiful place was supposed to add to the couple's special day, but Elizabeth's happiness soon turned to sadness when, after her husband took off somewhere in the chateau, she went looking for him. She found him embraced in the arms of another woman. Her dream man, she realized, was nothing but an unfaithful louse. Her world—and all her dreams of marital bliss—crumbled before her very eyes. So distraught was she at the revelation of her unfaithful husband, and so soon after they took their vows, that Elizabeth decided her life wasn't worth living anymore. After all, she thought, how would she again find happiness when she thought she already had found her true love? And now this!

She made a drastic decision that would end her life, but seemingly not her misery. Elizabeth's sad spirit has been rumored to haunt the chateau ever since that fateful day in the 1930s when she made a permanent decision about a temporary problem and allegedly flung herself from her room's window.

Her spirit has reportedly been seen in the hallways and kitchen but, perhaps ironically, rarely in Room 310, from which she jumped out the window. It also is rumored that she hides in the third-floor linen closet, where the sounds of crying and moaning have been heard. Even in death, she's not the happiest of souls, often taking her frustrations out on others—she has been known to throw objects at unwary staff members or visitors.

If you visit the chateau, don't worry about checking into her room, because even though she might be ornery, she does respect the privacy of the hotel's guests. Whenever someone checks into Room 310, the spirit leaves. It's at those times, when her room is being occupied, that she has been seen in the hallways or elsewhere in the chateau.

The Chateau at Oregon Caves is spacious but cozy, resembling a large cabin with log posts and beams and rock fireplaces. Its location is perfect for the nature lover, with wilderness all around. The stream actually runs through the hotel, and its façade is shingled with tree bark. If the stories are true, it's no wonder Elizabeth's spirit may want to remain here.

Middle Oregon

FROM GHOSTLY FACES IN THE WINDOWS OF AN OLD MANSION TO STRANGE lights in the sky over Bend, this section covers the otherworldly in middle Oregon, which, if you looked at a map, would in this context include the counties of Hood River, Wasco, Sherman, Gilliam, Morrow, Jefferson, Wheeler, Crook, Deschutes, and Lake—places where there is plenty to do in the outdoors and where, with its quiet charm, the past and present come alive to create a whole new history of its own.

While here, especially at night, be sure to look heavenward: You just might see strange lights in the sky. The area seems to have a lot of UFO activity. But upward isn't the only place where you might see odd lights. There's also a cemetery in this region of the state where blue orbs have been seen at night. If the lights aren't ghost activity, what are they?

There also are strange highways and streets in the area that you'd probably rather not traverse by yourself. You've come this far, though. Don't get scared now, because as we've seen up to this point, such things are common occurrence in the Beaver State.

Faces in the Windows

Something else that has been on my mind is the question of how ghost stories get started. The simplest of answers is that someone, at one time or another, experienced a paranormal or unexplained event at a location and later told the story, which spread among others and became something of an urban legend. Sometimes, as you've seen, the stories become embellished. But what are other ways that stories begin to be circulated? Perhaps a tragic crime was committed at a location, or maybe a suicide, sparking the assumption that the place then must be haunted by either the curse of the crime or the spirits of the dead. Maybe a house with its dark windows and falling shingles looks spooky and the neighborhood children tell tall tales of it being haunted by unwieldy ghosts, even though such entities may not really exist in the place. However the stories begin, one thing is for sure: There is no dearth of folktales, urban legends, and the allegedly true stories of ghosts and strange phenomena.

What's difficult is proving that the stories are true. Likewise, it's difficult to prove that they are not true. So much of what becomes folktale and legend are but fragments of an often much larger or complex story, one whose details have been lost through time or careless oral historians—the common people who pass along the stories.

I could easily have added to the stories about a supposedly haunted house that I wrote about in my book on south-central Idaho haunts, but I did not. For the front cover image of my book *Ghosts of Idaho's Magic Valley: Hauntings and Lore*, the publisher used a photograph I took of one of the book's primary haunts, an old homestead along the Oregon Trail in Twin Falls County. If you look at the cover, it looks as if a human figure is peering out one of the lower windows near the home's porch.

At first, I thought that perhaps the publisher added the face digitally in an effort to make the image of the house look spookier than it really was, but then I retrieved the original image from my own files and also thought I had captured something paranormal. There, in the original image, I saw the anomaly. I zoomed in on the supposed face—and my heart sank. It wasn't a supernatural image, but rather a flier taped to the window, announcing tours of the historic

grounds. From a distance, however, it truly resembled a face peering out the window.

Maybe the faces seen in the windows of the Thomas McCann House in Bend, Oregon, really are those of living spirits. Faces in the windows are just some of the stories associated with the historic mansion that was built in 1915 at 440 Northwest Congress Street. The house, also known as the Congress House and now listed on the National Register of Historic Places, was built for the vice president and general manager of the Shevlin-Hixon Lumber Company, a position Thomas McCann held for several years.

The cozy-looking mansion-style house is surrounded by tall trees, which could add to the stories of ghosts because to some eyes it just might "look that way." Websites such as BendSource.com and TheShadowLands.net say the house might be cursed, noting that many people over the years who have moved into the mansion have had unexpected tragedy befall them. Are these just stories because someone, at one time, thought they saw faces in the upper windows? Or is there more truth to the stories than legend?

Spooky Streets

There are some roads better left untraveled, and the stretch of U.S. Highway 97, between Culver and Crooked River Bridge, is one such road. According to legend, it is haunted by some things that are more unexplainable than mere ghosts. Like what, you ask? How about cows, for instance, that suddenly appear on the road with glowing eyes?

These bovines aren't your everyday, run-of-the-mill dairy or beef cows, but creatures that find pasture in a more ethereal plane of existence. Of course, more rational beings might say the unearthly glow is caused by headlights shining on the cattle's eyes. That is something to think about, but then again, there are other stories about phantom shades of human spirits that walk the highway, zombie-like, in what seems to be an endless search for recovery and redemption. I don't think that vision is caused by headlights.

There apparently have been many car accidents on this stretch of highway, perhaps leading to the stories of it being haunted. Maybe it is not only people but also cows that have been hit on the road, their spirits returning to the scene of their earthly demise. Pay close attention when traveling this highway—first and foremost for safety, but also to keep a sharp eye for late-night phantoms. If you see one of them sticking out its thumb for a ride, you might want to think again before slowing down and offering a pickup. As for those cows with their glowing eyes, don't stop to offer any hay. Just keep on driving away, far away. . .

Another paved roadway, Northwest Oregon Avenue in Bend, supposedly has its share of strange occurrences. Strange lights that suddenly appear out of nowhere, phantom footsteps heard slapping the pavement, and ghostly voices that come from nowhere are but a few of the unexplained phenomena that happen on this street in middle Oregon.

Why the street is haunted is anybody's guess, but there are a couple of assumptions. One is that events from the past that took place in this area dictate the strange occurrences today. The phantom sounds could be either those of a residual nature or from intelligent beings trying to communicate with living, sensitive souls. The second assumption—and in the realm of the paranormal, an assumption is all we can call it—is that the street serves as some type of conduit or circuit for paranormal activity. In some theories, moving water serves as a conduit for such activity because spirits need energy to manifest themselves, whether as orbs, moving lights, or full-bodied apparitions.

Do they also need energy to create sounds, even if it's the slapping of footfalls on pavement? Who's to say? But not far from the northeast end of the street (it runs southwest to northeast) are the Deschutes River and nearby Drake Park, which means there is plenty of water in the area to help ignite the faintest ghost.

If anything, it gives food for thought. What else would cause phantom activity in an otherwise busy thoroughfare? Your guess is as good as mine. It's best to travel the street on foot if you're seeking ghostly activity. Keep a sharp ear for those otherworldly sounds. Who knows—you just might encounter a real phantom.

UFOs over Middle Oregon

Ever since mankind turned his head heavenward, he has wondered what lies beyond the starry night sky. The earth itself, both on dry land and in the ocean depths, is filled with marvelous creations.

Why couldn't the rest of the universe have similar, albeit different, creations? Much like our mortal sphere and the world of spirits that sometimes cross-connect, earth's boundaries are at times broken by beings allegedly from other worlds. Sometimes abductions occur, but more often than not strange lights are seen by unsuspecting witnesses who look to the night sky.

The mystery of UFOs has haunted mankind for centuries. "UFOs have always been with us—and they're still with us today," writes Mack Maloney in his book *UFOs in Wartime: What They Didn't Want You to Know*, a classy volume that describes the many UFO sightings that have happened during times of conflict, from Constantine to the Persian Gulf. "They frequently appear at night, sometimes in groups, but mostly just as one or two. They can fly faster and maneuver unlike any man-made aerial machine. They are generally benign, though they may or may not abduct humans in order to see what makes us tick. And they seem to be able to come and go at will, anytime, anywhere."

Even the Bible mentions strange objects that appear seemingly out of nowhere in a quiet sky. Perhaps one of the most popular biblical stories to which many UFO buffs refer, saying that Planet Earth has been watched by alien eyes for centuries or even millennia, is that of Ezekiel and his chariot of fire. The prophet's eyewitness account, recorded in about 539 BC, reads in part:

> And I looked, and, behold, a whirlwind came out of the north, a great cloud, and a fire infolding itself, and a brightness was about it, and out of the midst thereof as the colour of amber, out of the midst of the fire. Also out of the midst thereof came the likeness of four living creatures. And this was their appearance; they had the likeness of a man. . . .
>
> Now as I beheld the living creatures, behold one wheel upon the earth by the living creatures, with his four faces. The appearance of the wheels and their work was like unto the colour of a beryl: and they four had one likeness: and their appearance and their work was as it were a wheel in the middle of a wheel. When they went, they went upon their four sides: and they turned not when they went.
>
> As for their rings, they were so high that they were dreadful; and their rings were full of eyes round about them four. And when the living creatures went, the wheels went by them: and when the living creatures were lifted up from the earth, the wheels were lifted

up. Whithersoever the spirit was to go, they went, thither was their spirit to go; and the wheels were lifted up over against them: for the spirit of the living creature was in the wheels. When those went, these went; and when those stood, these stood; and when those were lifted up from the earth, the wheels were lifted up over against them: for the spirit of the living creature was in the wheels.

And the likeness of the firmament upon the heads of the living creature was as the colour of the terrible crystal, stretched forth over their heads above. And under the firmament were their wings straight, the one toward the other: every one had two, which covered on this side, and every one had two, which covered on that side, their bodies. And when they went, I heard the noise of their wings, like the noise of great waters, as the voice of the Almighty, the voice of speech, as the noise of an host: when they stood, they let down their wings.

—Ezekiel 1:4–5, 15–25.

While UFO enthusiasts hail the prophet's description as one of the world's greatest accounts of an encounter with extraterrestrial life, those who are religious attribute it simply to a heavenly vision, with the strange creature descriptions symbolic of the glories and endless creations of God.

There is indeed something magical about imagining that creatures beyond the outer limits have an interest in us. But if indeed they do, what is that interest and what is their purpose in visiting our solar system or our planet? Why do alien abductions allegedly occur? Are those who visit from the outer limits malevolent beings, as depicted in H. G. Wells's *War of the Worlds*, or are they benevolent creatures like the friendly E.T. in Steven Spielberg's fairytale? And, we can't help but wonder, what do aliens look like? Do they look like something out of a sci-fi movie or do they resemble us? Will we ever know? Are they even really aliens, or are they demons in disguise?

Whatever the answers might be, a number of unidentified flying craft have been reported in the deep skies over the Beaver State, including several in Bend and other areas of central Oregon. Here are a few as reported to the National UFO Reporting Group:

August 3, 2011: A military aircraft seemed to be chasing a UFO one night around 11:30 P.M. between Lakeview and Adel, according to witnesses who saw the strange chase. Two brothers first saw the three orange lights hanging stationary in the sky. At first, they thought the lights were radio towers, but more lights soon appeared with the first three, and then they started moving. "Each object would fade out slowly and then quickly snap back into view, but when their lights would snap back on they were typically in a very different part of the sky. After a while other similar objects seemed to show up and then later disappear." About two minutes after they disappeared, military aircraft showed up. "One of the plans [*sic*] seemed to go invisible right before it got over our heads and it stayed invisible until it was almost over the horizon," the witnesses reported. Were the lights in fact from military planes or something from the outer limits?

August 13, 2011: A large triangular light appeared in the skies over Mount Hood on a late summer evening. A second, smaller, cigar-shaped light then appeared and traveled toward the larger light. The triangular object, according to the witness who reported it, looked as if it had "rounded corners." The lights didn't last long before vanishing from the sky.

September 25, 2011: "Pulsing, rotating red and green lights with flashes of white light" were seen over Bend by a witness who reported that the lights had been seen for several months just after sunset in the northeast sky. At first, the lights seemed to remain stationary, causing some to consider if this was not from a more natural phenomena in our galaxy, such as the star Sirius. But, according to the witness, the lights rotated red and green.

August 13, 2012: A mother and daughter were in the family's yard one night, watching shooting stars, when suddenly there appeared a golden-orange-colored orb moving from the east toward the bay. The mother at first thought the object was a plane, but the light that emanated from the object was "much larger than a landing light," she reported, "not the right color, and there was no sound." The light seemed to move slowly and, to the surprise of the two backyard stargazers, they saw a second light emerge from the first. Before long, several more lights appeared out of the first and others from seemingly out of nowhere. Some of the lights would "turn off" for a few seconds before turning back on. The witness said this was not a "blinking" motion, but a distinct turning-off motion. After a couple of minutes, the light disappeared and a loud rumbling was heard.

December 30, 2012: On a snowy night, an orange light was seen flying beneath the clouds from north to south. It continued in the same direction for what appeared to be a few miles before shooting straight up into the clouds and disappearing from sight. Shortly thereafter, a red light appeared and followed the same course, "bobbing back and forth a bit." There was no sound with these appearances, and after the lights went into the clouds, the two witnesses who saw them said they never reappeared.

December 31, 2012: A witness reported seeing two bright orange and red lights in the night sky over Bend. The lights appeared to remain stationary at first, but after a couple of minutes they seemed to move straight up until, one by one, they disappeared from sight. Several other witnesses reported having also seen orange and red lights behave in much the same way.

The Blue Orbs of Pilot Butte Cemetery

Whenever the topic of ghosts and paranormal activity is brought up, you can bet that somewhere in the conversation will arise the issue of orbs—that bane of hard-nosed investigators of the unknown. That is exactly what orbs are: the unknown. Some consider orbs to be nothing more than illusionary dust particles, moisture, or light anomalies caught on film or by digital means. They do not have anything to do with energy, spirits, or the netherworld. Others believe orbs are manifestations of ghostly presences, perhaps not ghosts themselves but the manifestations of nearby spirit beings.

The ongoing controversy became more heated with the advent of digital technology, when many more orb anomalies were picked up by cameras. I fall in the middle area, or as *The Twilight Zone* producer and screenwriter Rod Serling would say, somewhere "between light and shadow, between science and superstition." I believe that a great many orbs, defined by their photographers as paranormal, are nothing more than moisture or dust caught on the lens or in the air. But not all of them. I believe there's also a group that are, at the very least, unexplained phenomena, and just maybe they are the mild manifestations of unseen, but sometimes felt, ghostly presences.

I had an experience one day that made me come to this latter conclusion. A number of orbs have been caught on film at a particular house I had visited in Utah, but nothing quite as unnerving as one day after a funeral when a cluster of them appeared in a digital photo. A sequence of shots was taken at the same angle in the same room, one right after another. No orbs in photo one. No orbs in photos two, three, or four. But in photo five there appeared a cluster of orbs, grouped together as if forming a face. How could that happen, if not something beyond our normal, mortal reasoning?

This anecdote serves as background for the strange phenomena at Pilot Butte Cemetery. The graveyard, established in 1913, includes forty acres. Fourteen acres are developed and, according to the Bend city website, maintained by personnel from the Street Division. It is at this hallowed ground—wherein the bodies of deceased residents have been laid to rest—that strange, unexplained lights have been seen floating among the grave markers. Most of the lights are described as blue orbs. In some paranormal circles, orbs of different colors mean different things. Blue, for instance, might mean either a calming presence or the presence of a spiritual guide.

"Moving mystery lights that seem to react intelligently to people are an old phenomenon, too. Some may be 'earth lights' caused by natural energy or marshy gases. But others are not so easily explained away," writes Rosemary Ellen Guiley on her website, VisionaryLiving.com. "Mystery lights are often seen in paranormal 'hot zones' such as the Skinwalker Ranch area in Utah, the Bridgewater Triangle in Massachusetts, and many more locations. Some extraterrestrial contactees associate them with UFO activity."

Like my experience with orbs some years ago, the phenomena witnessed at Pilot Butte Cemetery seems to be one of those happenings that just can't be explained away or tucked into a nice little box. Those who've investigated the old graveyard say they also have caught EVP recordings—phantom voices captured on digital recorders.

If you visit, don't trespass at night, and be sure to respect the property and the grave markers. After all, this is the physical home for some eternal beings.

Eastern Oregon

No matter where you go in Oregon, chances are you'll be in a city, town, forest, or on a beach that has some sort of paranormal or strange story associated with it. While the majority of this book's haunted locations seem to be in the northwestern part of the state, there are other ghosts and strange creatures that have made it their business to haunt the opposite end, in the Beaver State's eastern region. Here you'll encounter the ghost of a young woman who haunts an otherwise family-friendly park; specters of an old mine; spirits of a real ghost town; strange swamp creatures and those a little more hairy; and a homey, haunted hotel. Eastern Oregon, for the purposes of this book, comprises the seven counties of Morrow, Umatilla, Union, Wallowa, Grant, Baker, Harney, and Malheur. It doesn't have any ocean and the climate is milder than its western counterpart, but it's a beautiful region in its own right—one with ghosts, strange creatures, and weird history.

The Ghost Woman of Candy Cane Park

There's a small park on the corner of Twelfth Street and J Avenue in Le Grande, where the bars of a swing set are painted candy-cane-striped red and white. It is fitting because the park itself is named Candy Cane Park, a nearly two-acre complex that includes

a playground, picnic tables, benches, tall shade trees, a basketball court, and a small baseball field. Families come here to picnic and play, and for most visitors the experience is a pleasant one. A few, however, have become unnerved by an unexpected visitor: the spirit of a young lady who has been seen weeping in the park.

One of the darker stories about the park is that a murder was committed here long ago, and the victim's spirit has not been able to rest ever since. According to the story, she was killed by a man wielding an ax who tried to cut off her head. She was found alive in the park, but died shortly after. Her spirit, as sad it must be from the memory of the tragedy, does not always weep. Sometimes it has been seen swinging on the swing set or sitting on a park bench, as casual as can be, before fading into oblivion as if she never existed.

As folktales often go, there is much missing from the story. Why, for instance, was the woman at the park? Was she there by herself and a maniac came upon her? Or did she go there to meet a man, perhaps an estranged lover? Was the one she went to meet her killer, or was it someone else while she sat waiting? And why does the woman's spirit continue to appear at the scene of the alleged crime? She is not always seen crying, so what is her reason for visiting at those times when her spirit seems to be enjoying itself on the bench or swing set?

If nothing else, it tells us that spirits seem to enjoy some of the same activities that their mortal counterparts enjoyed in mortality. That makes sense, doesn't it? If we are eternal beings, why would our attitudes and enjoyments change after death? Apparently, if the story of the ghost woman of Candy Cane Park is true, they don't.

The next time you visit Candy Cane Park, keep a sharp eye out for that ephemeral young lady, who, for one reason or another, seems to have ties to the place of her earthly demise. Maybe the park was a happy place for her before the tragedy, and that's why sometimes she's seen without tears on her cheeks.

Ol' Malheur Butte

Something strange goes on at Malheur Butte, a volcano that was active some 15 million to 20 million years ago. But just because the volcano is extinct doesn't mean its surroundings are quiet; in fact, the area is quite active with geothermal activity, as seen from the many hot springs in the vicinity. At least one business is said to use the geothermal energy produced here.

Long before any businesses were built here, the native Indians used the five-hundred-foot-tall mountain to watch for wagon trains along the Oregon Trail. Who were these white folk? the Indians wondered as they spied the worn travelers, sometimes coming in hoards to Oregon Country. If they could secure goods from the emigrants, all the better.

Indians weren't the only ones who, at one time or another, used the ragged butte for shady purposes. The site allegedly has been a favorite spot for those practicing witchcraft. Curses, spells, and sacrifices have been committed here, according to the legend, their dark deeds imprinted into the soil and atmosphere of the area. If you visit and sense something oddly chilling, it might mean you're sensitive to those dark imprints. Is the land cursed? Who's to say, but some call it unholy ground. As old as it is, we can only wonder what other historic imprints are left at this iconic, extinct volcano.

Ghosts of the Crescent Mine

Mines of all varieties pockmark much of the western United States in testament to man's quest for exploration and riches. Being a miner is tough, thankless work that many times in history has taken more than it has given. In the twenty-first century, man is still digging underground in search of Mother Earth's precious bounty. Success has come to many, but distress, disaster, and death have come to others. Families of mine workers are left behind to mourn loved ones lost in accidents underground, and the very mines in which workers toiled are left as grave markers. Just take a look at the United States Mine Rescue Association website (www.usmra.com/Mine_Disasters) to view a list of mine disasters from early 1839 to the present. It's a disheartening look at this risky but worthy profession.

Sometimes these very mines, dark with forgotten light, are haunted by the spirits of the lives they took. Enter Crescent Mine near Sumpter in northeast Oregon, one of several mines that dot the Beaver State's eastern half.

In early 2013, the Syfy Network aired a new show called *Ghost Mine*, in which paranormal investigators search the dark bellies of the earth to uncover riches and ghosts. The first season took place in and around Sumpter—a logical choice for the show's setting, as Sumpter was the largest mining town in the area from the late nineteenth through early twentieth century. According to a January 4, 2013, article by Jayson Jacoby in the *Baker City Herald*, "Sumpter, which celebrated its 150th birthday this year, reached a population of about 3,000 during the peak of the hard-rock mining period in the decade or so before the First World War. But the mines mainly played out, and then a massive fire in August 1917 destroyed almost all of the town's buildings."

The town today is a local tourist spot, where an abundant list of outdoor recreation activities is the main draw. People like to visit the Sumpter Valley Dredge, "a monstrous machine that scoured the Sumpter Valley for gold before shutting down in 1954." It is now the centerpiece of the town's state park.

Mine owner Larry Overman told *Ghost Mine* that one of his crew walked off the job because of the paranormal happenings in the mine. Shadow figures, strange EVPs, and cold spots are some of the things that have been discovered. Investigators have captured EVP recordings that say "I'm lost" with a Chinese accent. One of the hosts of *Ghost Mine* asked the spirit if something bad happened in the mine. The answer was "yes." Shadow figures reportedly have been seen at camp, equipment malfunctions for no apparent reason, and items have been known to mysteriously disappear or be found misplaced. There's even a place inside the mines called "The Ballroom," where time allegedly is warped. You may think you're in there for just a few minutes, when actually hours have passed. Later, the hosts investigated the Sumpter Valley Dredge and claimed they captured the image of a full-bodied apparition of a miner named Joe.

There are also all sorts of superstitions associated with the mine, as there are with others. For instance, it is believed that Tommy-knockers—also known as goblins or sprites—live in the deep tunnels, guiding miners to the riches by knocking on the tunnel walls. It also is believed that if a worker whistles in the mine, it drives away the "good-luck spirit" and calls attention to the evil spirits that lurk underground.

Women, especially redheaded women, have been considered bad luck in mines and omens of death. Redheads in general have apparently gotten a bad rap in some superstitious circles throughout the ages. One nautical superstition is that redheads were bad luck aboard sailing vessels. (It was said that the bad luck could be averted, however, if the redhead was spoken to first before the redhead spoke.) In the late sixteenth century, it was believed the fat of a redheaded male was a necessary ingredient in poison. Red hair was considered an abnormality in Germanic culture from 1483 to 1784, when thousands were stripped and searched for any form of the devil's mark. Folklore in Liverpool, England, says that meeting a redhead at the beginning of a journey is an omen of bad luck. And if a redhead entered a mine—especially a redheaded woman— bad luck was inevitable.

It is unclear what presences haunt the mine or how many, but it doesn't seem to be a place of rest for the entities that lurk here, nor for the miners who work in its deep darkness. On theory: maybe these spirits found something of great worth in the mines and haunt it in an effort to distract others from uncovering their precious find.

The Ghosts of Granite

Something that distinguishes the West from other areas of the country are its ghost towns, usually once-busy gold-mining towns that, after their booms, dried up and drifted into history. These towns, abandoned by all but memory and historical markers, are interesting places to catch a glimpse of the past. Free of their human inhabitants, or at least mostly so, ghost towns often are places where, true to their name, spirits linger. A few ghost towns exist in Oregon, including Granite, located about fifteen miles northwest of Sumpter in the northeastern corner of Baker County.

Granite came to life after Jack Long, a prospector, got his mule stuck in the mud while packing a load of whiskey on July 4, 1862. After he pulled the animal from the mud, Long found gold dust on his mule's hooves. He immediately staked his claim, thinking he had found his riches. This quickly drew the attention of others, and before long a town was being built.

Long originally wanted to name the town Independence, after the holiday on which he discovered the gold, but postal authorities negated that idea, saying there already was such a town. It was instead named Granite after the abundance of that rock in the region. By 1900, the town boasted a drugstore, livery stable, post office, five saloons, three stores, two hotels, and a population of around five thousand people. More than half of the town's residents were Chinese, and most of the population was male. The forty-two-room Grand Hotel served meals until the late 1930s; it was destroyed in 1943. The post office closed fourteen years later, in 1957.

Slowly but eventually, the same curse that befell all ghost towns came to Granite. The mines dried up, people moved away, and buildings were either torn down or left uninhabited—except, that is, for the few people who still make Granite their home today, and the alleged ghosts who eventually moved in and still linger here.

Step back into the past by visiting this scenic mountain ghost town in beautiful eastern Oregon and see for yourself why it just might be haunted by more than a memory. Watch for faces in old building windows, listen for the moaning sounds that might be more than just the wind, and keep a sharp eye for old-timers dressed in period miner gear. Oh, and don't be surprised if you smell cigar smoke and whiskey, just as if they were in the here and now, even though none of that exists in the old buildings today.

Smile, You're on Graveyard Camera

A photographer using a time-lapse camera got more than he expected when he set up his camera on a summer evening in 2013 in the Old Pioneer Cemetery in Milton-Freewater, Oregon. Nathan Ziegler placed his camera on a tripod and set it to snap a frame every thirty seconds. In a video of Ziegler discussing his find, he says the first photo was taken at 8:13 P.M. and the last a little before 10 P.M. that same night. After returning to the cemetery to retrieve his equipment, he went home and downloaded the photos to his computer. He didn't notice anything out of the ordinary until the next morning, when he again reviewed the photographs.

Watching the slideshow like a mini movie, as posted on YouTube, you notice clouds float by in the evening sky, the prairie grass sway in the breeze and then, in just one frame, the dark humanlike shadow figure of "something" to the right of a tree. Ziegler then zooms in on the video, showing the strange figure close up. It seems very much like a human, except its head appears elongated, resembling, at least in my mind, that of a Kokopelli fertility god or something you might see in a Hollywood science-fiction movie.

Often, photographers who've unexpectedly captured something paranormal with their cameras try to explain the mystery, saying there must be a logical explanation for the image: a dust particle, drop of moisture, or odd lighting. But in his video presentation of the image, Ziegler simply says: "I still haven't figured this one out."

Since the camera was timed to take pictures every thirty seconds, could someone have walked into the frame within that time, and then back out before the camera took the next picture? It is not impossible, perhaps, but unlikely. Or is there something more paranormal involved? It is a strange coincidence indeed, because from a viewer's standpoint you might wonder how a person could make the trek from one end of the frame to the other, where the tree was standing, in thirty seconds. Could there have been a person behind the tree when Ziegler set up his camera, popping out only sometime later after the photographer left the cemetery?

Reason would say yes, that something akin to this must have happened. But upon reexamining the picture itself, it begins to appear otherwise very quickly. The image, while it does resemble a human being, also in many ways looks like a sinister or unnatural image of something humanlike, but not quite human. Again, that elongated head, the posture of the body, and the short, stubby legs all lead the viewer to believe it is a creature not of the mortal kind. Perhaps strange things as this should come as no surprise, since Ziegler was recording in a cemetery.

The Old Pioneer Cemetery, which sits atop a hill overlooking the city of Milton-Freewater, is the eternal resting place for the bodies of some of Oregon's early inhabitants. Several graves date back to 1878. Many of them are unknown; several were unearthed in the 1930s but still have not been identified. Some of the skulls, however, were discovered to be Indian, while others were from white men, causing some to speculate that perhaps the place was the site of a confrontation in Oregon's early days. Does the cemetery sit atop a former battlefield? It very well could, because according to the Findagrave.com website, the graveyard also was the site of an original stagecoach road, which Indians often would attack.

Could the strange figure that Ziegler caught on camera be a spirit who roams here, perhaps belonging to one of the area's earliest pioneer settlers? And then there's the question of shadow figures. What are they, and is the figure on Ziegler's camera one of them? Of course, like Ziegler, we do not know and cannot say with authority what was captured digitally. Perhaps it was something discussed here, or maybe it was something else paranormal for which there is yet no human explanation.

That's the tricky part about studying the strange and unexplained—it often remains unexplained, even after countless theories have been proposed. Will we ever know all the mysteries of this earth and what lies beyond the grave? Perhaps, but it just might not be until we ourselves have passed beyond the veil.

The Wallowa Lake Monster

It's difficult to tell for sure, but it's believed the monster that haunts Wallowa Lake might have horns atop its head. The creature, which reportedly has been seen in the cold lake since before the white man appeared in Oregon Country, is described as resembling a Chinese dragon, with several humps on its back.

Wally, as the creature sometimes is called by the locals, once pulled an Indian brave under the water to his drowning death. As the story goes, a warrior from the Nez Perce tribe unexpectedly disturbed the creature while venturing high into the mountains that surround the lake. The beast was startled by the unexpected intrusion and quickly moved down the mountain, plunging into the lake. That didn't stop the young warrior from pursuing the monster into the water, thinking he'd receive great honors from his tribe if he captured or killed such a creature. He could never get close enough, however, for every time it looked as if he would, the monster would submerge.

Finally giving up, the warrior headed back to shore, but it already was too late. Before the warrior could make more than just a few strokes toward shore, he felt a tug on his legs. His warrior comrades, who stood on shore watching the episode, witnessed the disturbing scene as the young warrior suddenly was pulled under the water. That was the last they saw of him, but not the last they saw of the creature, which supposedly haunted Indian tribes for years to come.

"In 1885, a prospector, who wished to keep his identity a secret, was about midway across the lake when he saw an animal about fifty yards to the right of his boat," reads an article about the monster on UnknownExlorers.com. "The animal reared its head and neck out of the water about 10 feet, paused, then quickly dove back into the water."

Reports of sightings have continued into modern times, and there have been many theories as to what the creature might be. It is all conjecture, however, because no one knows for sure. According to the same article, witness reports have said the creature sighted was anywhere from eight feet to one hundred feet long, quite a span. As of yet, no physical evidence of Wally has been found. But much like ghosts, the lack of physical evidence does not prove that there isn't such a thing as the Wallowa Lake Monster. Just because you might not have seen it yourself doesn't mean that such a creature doesn't truly exist.

Both the lake and the surrounding wilderness seem to attract the attention of other strangeness. Several reports of UFOs list Wallowa Lake as a popular location for such sightings, and a clan of Sasquatch is believed to haunt the scenic woods. Bigfoot sightings in the area have stretched back for years. In 1970, a traveler parked alongside the road for a nap in his camper. Before long, he was awakened by something large and heavy running nearby, grunting and shaking the camper as it did. The witness reported a rancid stench in the air at the time, a common attribute of Bigfoot encounters.

Apparently that wasn't the first time the creature unnerved a lake visitor. A gentleman who worked in a nearby gas station told the traveler there had been similar reports by others. Other sightings of the infamous creature have been related over the years on or near Wallowa Lake Road.

The Swamp Thing

Sometimes the presence of the supernatural or earthly strange is not seen, but rather heard. Bigfoot allegedly is heard on the Umatilla Indian Reservation near Pendleton. Reports of the strange sounds began in November 2012 and are believed to originate in a swamp on the reservation. The *Oregonian* reported that the cries range from "high-pitched screams to basso profundo roars."

The sounds cause hairs to stand on end and unnerve those who live in the tribal housing unit near the swamp, such as Sylvia Minthorn, who was interviewed by the newspaper in early 2013.

Some residents thought the sounds might be coyotes or foxes playing or hunting at night, while others believed the disturbing noises come from something more ominous, such as Bigfoot. One belief was that they were the cries of a young Sasquatch who became separated from his family.

It wasn't the first time that such a creature was believed to haunt the 178,000-acre reservation that includes part of northeastern Oregon's Blue Mountains. No one was able to pinpoint the exact location from whence the sounds came, but the swamp in question borders the old reservation community of Mission. The mountains around the reservation have been a "hot spot" of Bigfoot activity since 1966, the *Oregonian* reported, when a cyclist named Pete Luther from Walla Walla, Washington, found nineteen-inch footprints along Tiger Canyon Road, just north of the reservation near the Oregon–Washington border.

If the legend is true and a Bigfoot clan really does roam the Blue Mountains, they've picked a beautiful and expansive place to call home. The mountain range, which is more than four thousand square miles and part of the larger Columbia River Plateau, stretches east and southeast of Pendleton to the Snake River along the Oregon–Idaho border. It was a formidable obstacle to immigrants traveling the Oregon Trail in the mid- to late 1800s and was the last they had to cross before reaching their destination of either southeast Washington or Oregon's Willamette Valley. The Umatilla wilderness is the smallest wilderness in northeast Oregon, encompassing 20,114 acres in Umatilla and Union Counties and teeming with forest wildlife—and, if the legend is true, Bigfoot.

But that's another question: Is Bigfoot considered wildlife? In some respects, perhaps, but the creature more appropriately is called Sasquatch, an anglicized derivative of the word *Sesquac*, meaning "wild man." Bigfoot, Sasquatch, and Yeti—a Tibetan name that means "magical creature"—are all different names for the same type of ape-like creature, or wild man, that has stalked America's backwoods—and in the case of the Yeti, the rugged mountains of Tibet—for decades.

For at least four centuries, people have claimed to have seen hairy, manlike creatures stalk the forests of North America. Since 1810 when David Thompson, a surveyor and trader, spotted large footprints resembling human feet near the Columbia River Gorge, these strange creatures have been known as Bigfoot. It wasn't until the 1930s, however, that the idea of Bigfoot became legendary in American culture when sightings of the alleged beast began to be reported all over the country, from the Florida Everglades to the Pacific Northwest. What were the screeching sounds heard on the Umatilla Indian Reservation in late 2012? Was it Bigfoot or something more natural, like a coyote? It is inconclusive, but this might help: Minthorn's uncle, Armand, said he found large, manlike footprints years ago, sixteen to eighteen inches long, while hunting in the mountains.

Haunting at Hot Lake Hotel

There's an old hotel in northeast Oregon that for years has been rumored to be haunted by at least one ghost, and possibly more than one. Rocking chairs move back and forth as if someone is sitting in them, but they are empty of human occupancy. The patter of small feet in the upstairs hallways makes it sound as if children are at play but, like the rocking chairs, the hallways are empty. A rough, strained woman's voice is heard whooshing through the dank air but—you guessed it—no one is there to claim the voice. These are just some examples of the strange occurrences that supposedly happen at the building once known as Hot Lake Hotel, now a privately owned bed-and-breakfast in Union County.

One of the more persistent stories of visible activity is that of an old gardener whose restless spirit still roams the grounds, spade in hand, long after his body was put into the grave. Some paranormal sites describe the facility as one of the most creepy, unnerving buildings in the Beaver State because of the spirits that allegedly call it their home. It apparently is not the original building to sit here, however. Built in 1864, the very first hotel constructed on the site became popular when it was rumored that the nearby hot springs contained healing powers. According to the stories, in 1917 Dr.

William T. Phy purchased the property and turned the building into a "modern" (for the time) medical sanitarium, capitalizing on the springs to draw patients. The building functioned as both hotel and hospital for the next fifteen years until a fire destroyed it in 1934. What was left was rebuilt, and the second facility served as several things over the years, including an asylum, a nursing home, and even a restaurant until the business plummeted and people moved on. The building sat unused during the late 1980s and early 1990s, which seems to be when the ghost stories started.

Don't seek out the ghosts for yourself. As with all places mentioned in this book, please respect private property and its owners.

The Sounds of Bigfoot

It's always an uncomfortable feeling when you believe you're being watched by unseen eyes. What's even more uncomfortable— frightening, even—is when those prying eyes are those of a mysterious creature belonging more to myth and legend than actual science. Welcome to Bigfoot territory in southeast Oregon.

In 1975, two elk hunters in the thick Oregon wilderness of the King Mountain area, about fifteen miles east of Highway 20 north of Burns in Harney County, were the victims of gooseflesh when they felt they were being followed by a creature they believed to be Sasquatch. The hunters, who reported their story on the Bigfoot Field Researchers Organization website, said they not only felt ill at ease, like someone was following them, but also heard actual noises that they had never heard before.

As the sun fell behind the ponderosa pine and Douglas fir that framed a narrow meadow, the two hunters were headed back to their pickup truck when they suddenly had the sensation of unseen eyes heavy upon them. What happened next increased their certainty that they were not alone in the woods. The hunters heard a loud scream, according to their report. "The sounds were continuous for at least five minutes," the report states, noting the noise came from behind the trees and that the hunters could hear something "banging on a tree and breaking branches."

The men, experienced hunters with ready rifles, found a boulder to hide behind and waited for the creature to show itself. It never did. "We were pretty scared by this time," they wrote. Their pickup was still about a half mile away, but they made it to the cab and drove off, setting up camp about fifteen miles away from where they heard the unnerving noises. The hunters say the sighting—err, hearing—happened in a relatively flat area at an elevation of about seven thousand feet. The creature apparently followed them, for the report next states that the hunters heard "something" circle their campsite about five different times. They never did see what made the sounds, only stating that it seemed to be "large and heavy."

That's the thing with some Bigfoot stories: They leave more mystery to the imagination than explanation. Did these hunters hear the sounds of a Bigfoot or could the heavy walking have been from an elk, moose, or bear? What about the scream they heard earlier in the evening? Was it from an unknown wild creature or was it an elk butting its antlers on a tree trunk? Or was what they heard truly the cry of a Bigfoot or perhaps another creature that no one—not even the scientific community—can prove truly exists? Those who've had their own encounters with the legendary monster no doubt will tend to believe the latter.

Another witness states that he heard the cries of a Bigfoot almost three decades later in the Call Meadow area, also in Harney County, while walking one evening along the edge of a road near pastureland. He described the commotion, which seemed to come from an undetected spot about one thousand feet away, as "a really horrible noise" that was difficult to describe. The witness explained that it sounded like the bellowing of a cow, but not a cow; like a hurtful scream, but not a scream; like a coyote, but not a coyote; and like a cougar, but not a cougar. One thing for sure, he explained, was that the indescribable, almost-anguished sound, which lasted for at least a minute and maybe longer, was loud and unnerving.

"I could see across the meadow, and kept watching while I headed back for the rig," the witness reported. "It was pretty scary, so I cut my walk short."

Bibliography

Books and Articles

Balzano, Christopher. *Ghostly Adventures: Chilling True Stories from America's Haunted Hot Spots.* New York: Fall River Press, 2008.

Cockle, Richard. "Bigfoot or animals? Strange sounds coming from the swamps on Umatilla Indian Reservation." The *Oregonian*, January 20, 2013.

Eufrasio, Al, and Jeff Davis. *Weird Oregon: Your Travel Guide to Oregon's Local Legends and Best Kept Secrets.* New York: Sterling Publishing, 2010.

Gorrow, Chelsea. "Flavel family mystery unsealed: Astoria officials find home in good shape, start work to resecure house." The *Daily Astorian*, updated December 11, 2013.

Guiley, Rosemary Ellen. *The Encyclopedia of Ghosts and Spirits.* New York: Checkmark Books, 1992.

Hagar, Sheila. "Mystery image appears in Milton-Freewater's Old Pioneer Cemetery: Photographer Nathan Ziegler is baffled by what he captured in a time-lapse photo session at dusk." *Union-Bulletin*, August 2, 2013.

Husk, Lee Lewis. "Haunted Oregon: From the Shanghai Tunnels to the high desert and inexplicable Vortex, something spirited this way comes." *1859: Oregon's Magazine*, September 1, 2012.

Jung, Helen. "Portland's buried truth: Historians say the story of the city's infamous Shanghai tunnels likely is a myth." The *Oregonian*, October 4, 2007.

Kershaw, Sarah. "Tourist Draw for Sale, With Mystery the Lure." The *New York Times*, September 19, 2003.

Maloney, Mack. *UFOs in Wartime: What They Didn't Want You to Know.* New York: Berkley, 2011.

Teeples, Joe. *Pacific Northwest Haunts: A Ghost Hunter's Field Guide.* Atglen, PA: Schiffer Publishing, 2010.

Weeks, Andy. *Ghosts of Idaho's Magic Valley: Hauntings and Lore.* Charleston, SC: The History Press, 2012.

———. *Haunted Idaho: Ghosts and Strange Phenomena of the Gem State.* Mechanicsburg, PA: Stackpole Books, 2013.

———. *Haunted Utah: Ghosts and Strange Phenomena of the Beehive State.* Mechanicsburg, PA: Stackpole Books, 2012.

Online Sources

"Abduction Reports." *UFO Watch.* www.ufowatch.com/default.asp. Retrieved September 2, 2013.

Adams, J. D. "Oregon Mysteries of the Sea." *Salem-News.com*, Jan. 11, 2011. http://www.salem-news.com/articles/january112011/oregon-coast.php. Retrieved March 17, 2013.

Albrecht, John Jr. "Strange shadowy figure caught on time-lapse camera in Oregon." *Akron Paranormal Examiner.* http://www.examiner.com/article/strange-shadowy-figure-captured-on-time-lapse-camera-oregon. Retrieved November 1, 2013.

Alexander, Patrick. "Creature suffers from child infestation." *The News Guard*, August 21, 2012. www.thenewsguard.com/news/article_9b266ae6-ebd2-11e1-893e-001a4bcf887a.html. Retrieved May 30, 2013.

"A look at Oregon's History." *Oregon-Coast Directory.* http://www.oregon-coastdirectory.com/history/history.htm. Retrieved March 17, 2013.

Barnard, Jeff. "Oregon Tourist Trap Holds Weird Twist." *ABC News*, March 11. http://abcnews.go.com/Travel/story?id = 119083&page = 1. Retrieved March 4, 2013.

Becker, Tim. "Astoria's Hess House haunted no more." *KOIN.com.* http://www.koin.com/on-koin/mystery-monday/astorias-hess-house-haunted-no-more. Retrieved October 7, 2013.

Bigfoot Encounters. www.bigfootencounters.com. Retrieved September 7, 2013.

"Bigfoot Filmed in Oregon!" *American Monsters.* http://www.americanmonsters.com/site/2010/09/bigfoot-filmed-in-oregon. Retrieved May 31, 2013.

"Bigfoot on the McKenzie River follow up." *The Caddis Fly: Oregon Fly Fishing Blog.* http://oregonflyfishingblog.com/2010/11/12/bigfoot-on-the-mckenzie-river-follow-up. Retrieved May 31, 2013.

Cheesman, Shannon L. "Is that a ghost that was caught on time-lapse?" *KATU.com*, August 2, 2013. http://www.katu.com/news/weird/-Did-a-timelapse-capture-a-ghost-218152901.html. Retrieved January 27, 2014.

"The Chetco County, Oregon Monster." *Bigfoot Encounter.* http://www.bigfootencounters.com/creatures/chetco.htm. Retrieved September 8, 2013.

Bibliography

Chilson, Jon. "Haunted Portland: Where Things go Bump in the Night." *Neighborhood Notes*, Oct. 19, 2010. http://www.neighborhoodnotes .com/news/2010/10/haunted_portland_where_things_go_bump_in_the _night/. Retrieved January 27, 2014.

The City of Lafayette, Oregon. http://www.ci.lafayette.or.us. Retrieved September 10, 2013.

Crater Lake Data Clearinghouse. http://oe.oregonexplorer.info/craterlake. Retrieved October 21, 2013.

Explore Eastern Oregon: Eastern Oregon Ghost Towns. http://www .visiteasternoregon.com/entry/eastern-oregon-ghost-towns. Retrieved February 25, 2013.

Fairies and Vampires. www.fairiesvampires.com/forum/topics/ghost-story -it-truethe. Retrieved January 27, 2014.

Finn, J. D. John. "The rowdy-but-golden past of almost-gold-town Granite." *Offbeat Oregon History*, May 5, 2009. http://www.offbeatoregon.com/ H105_Granite.htm. Retrieved February 25, 2013.

"Flavel House Museum." http://www.oldoregon.com/visitor-info/entry/ flavel-house-museum. Retrieved November 27, 2013.

Forest Grove, Oregon. http://www.forestgrove-or.gov/visitors/city -history.html. Retrieved November 11, 2013.

"Fort Clatsop." *The Oregon Encyclopedia.* http://www.oregonencyclopedia .org/entry/view/fort_clatsop_/. Retrieved November 19, 2012.

Frame 352: The Stranger Side of Sasquatch. http://paranormalbigfoot .blogspot.com/2009/02/ghost-in-conser-lake.html. Retrieved June 24, 2013.

"Glowing Sand on Oregon Coast, but Minus Tides a Mystery." *BeachConnection.net*, September 15, 2010. http://www.beachconnection.net/news/ glowmi091510_249.php. Retrieved August 22, 2013.

Guiley, Rosemary Ellen. "Reevaluating Orbs." *VisionaryLiving, Inc.* http://www.visionaryliving.com/2010/04/08/reevaluating-orbs. Retrieved October 16, 2013.

"Haunted Lighthouses along the Oregon Coast." *Romantic Oregon Coast Vacations.* http://www.romantic-oregon-coast.com/haunted-lighthouses .html. Retrieved November 10, 2012.

"Haunted Pub in Portland." *Travel Channel.* http://www.travelchannel.com/ video/haunted-pub-in-portland-11630. Retrieved September 4, 2013.

"Haunted Salem." *Salem Online History.* http://www.salemhistory.net/ brief_history/haunted_salem.htm. Retrieved July 8, 2013.

"Haunted Waldo." *Where's Waldo? A History of Waldo Hall and the Changing Role of Women at Oregon State.* http://scarc.library.oregonstate.edu/ omeka/exhibits/show/waldo/haunted/haunted. Retrieved January 27, 2014.

Hintz, Charlie. "Harry Flavel House in Astoria, Oregon." *Cult of Weird*, April 23, 2012. http://www.cultofweird.com/americana/flavel-house-astoria-oregon. Retrieved November 27, 2013.

"The History of Sumpter Oregon." *HistoricSumpter.com*. http://www .historicsumpter.com/sumpter-oregon-history.html. Retrieved June 1, 2013.

"Idaho Family has Bigfoot Encounter in Multnomah Falls, Oregon." *Bigfoot Encounters*. http://www.bigfootencounters.com/sbs/crowe02.htm. Retrieved October 12, 2013.

"Is The Chateau at Oregon Caves National Monument Haunted?" *National Parks Traveler*, October 28, 2009. http://www.nationalparkstraveler.com/ 2009/10/chateau-oregon-caves-national-monument-haunted4733. Retrieved September 9, 2013.

Jacoby, Jayson. "Ghostly Haunts Come to Life: TV show will mix ghost hunting, mining in Eastern Oregon." *Baker City Herald*, Jan. 4, 2013. http://www.columbian.com/news/2013/jan/04/ghostly-haunts-come -to-life. Retrieved January 27, 2014.

"Kennedy School." *McMenamins*. http://www.mcmenamins.com/427 -kennedy-school-home. Retrieved September 14, 2013.

"The Legendary White Eagle." *McMenamins*. http://www.mcmenamins .com/469-white-eagle-saloon-home. Retrieved June 15, 2013.

"Lewis & Clark: Fort Clatsop." *National Park Service*. http://www.nps.gov/ lecl/historyculture/fort-clatsop.htm. Retrieved November 5, 2013.

The Liberty Theater. http://www.liberty-theater.org. Retrieved November 17, 2012.

"The library at The Heathman Hotel, a Portland library experience for the Oregon intellectual traveler." *The Heathman Hotel*. http://portlandlibrary .heathmanhotel.com/aboutlibrary.aspx. Retrieved August 31, 2013.

Long, Greg. "The Monster of Conser Lake." *Oregonbigfoot.com*, October 1, 1996. http://www.oregonbigfoot.com/conserlake.html. Retrieved November 24, 2013.

"Malheur Butte." *TravelOregon.com*. http://traveloregon.com/see-do/ attractions/outdoors-nature/malheur-butte. Retrieved November 20, 2013.

"Mason's Cemetery." *RealHaunts.com*. http://www.realhaunts.com/united -states/masons-cemetery/#sthash.Z7DtdR94.dpuf. Retrieved August 23, 2013.

"May 11, 1950—McMinnville, Oregon, USA." *UFO Evidence*. http://www .ufoevidence.org/photographs/section/topphotos/photo301.htm. Retrieved August 17, 2013.

"McLoughlin House & Barclay House." *HauntedHouses.com*. http://www .hauntedhouses.com/states/or/mcloughlin_house.htm. Retrieved October 7, 2013.

The McLoughlin Memorial Association. http://www.mcloughlinhouse.org. Retrieved November 23, 2013.

"The Most Haunted Hotel in Portland, Oregon: The White Eagle Pub." *HauntedPlacestoGo.com*. http://www.haunted-places-to-go.com/most-haunted -hotel.html. Retrieved October 1, 2013.

Bibliography

Nochlin, Erica. "What was that in the sky? No, not the fireworks . . . that other thing." *KATU News*. http://www.katu.com/news/local/What-was-that-in-the-sky-No-not-the-fireworks-that-other-thing-214400431.html?tab = video&c = y. Retrieved July 17, 2013.

Nyholm, Christine Bude. "Haunted Heathman Hotel in Portland, OR," *Yahoo Voices*, Oct. 11, 2007. http://voices.yahoo.com/haunted-heathman-hotel-portland-or-589532.html. Retrieved January 27, 2014.

Oaks Park Amusement Park and Roller Rink. http://www.oakspark.com. Retrieved September 15, 2013.

"Old Pioneer Cemetery." *Find a Grave*. http://www.findagrave.com/cgi-bin/fg.cgi?page = cr&CRid = 2212525. Retrieved January 27, 2014.

Oregon Bigfoot.com. http://www.oregonbigfoot.com. Retrieved October 14, 2013.

"Oregon's Haunted Hotspots." *Carpe Noctem: Seize the Night*. http://www.carpenoctem.tv/hauntedhotspots/oregon/#sthash.OXfIrQTb.dpuf. Retrieved October 31, 2013.

"Oregon Legends: Sumpter—Queen City Ghost Town." *Legends of America*. http://www.legendsofamerica.com/or-sumpter.html. Retrieved June 1, 2013.

Owen, James. "New Species, 'Living Fossils,' Found in Atlantic." *National Geographic*, July 7, 2010. http://news.nationalgeographic.com/news/2010/07/photogalleries/100707-new-species-weird-deep-sea-atlantic-ocean-science-pictures. Retrieved January 27, 2014.

Owen, Rob. "'Ghost Mine': Digging for ghosts." The *Oregonian*, January 14, 2013. http://www.oregonlive.com/movies/index.ssf/2013/01/ghost_mine_digging_for_ghosts.html.Retrieved Nov. 10, 2013.

Pacific Paranormal Research Society. http://www.nwpprs.com/Ghost_Psychology.html . Retrieved October 31, 2013.

"Portland: Geography and Climate." *City-Data.com*. http://www.city-data.com/us-cities/The-West/Portland-Geography-and-Climate.html. Retrieved July 13, 2013.

Price, Niki. "Ghosts of the Oregon Coast." *Oregon Coast Today*. http://www.oregoncoasttoday.com/ghosts-of-the-oregon-coast.html. Retrieved October 27, 2013.

———. "Oregon Coast Shipwrecks." *Oregon Coast Today*. http://www.oregoncoasttoday.com/oregoncoastshipwrecks.html. Retrieved October 5, 2013.

"Red Hair Facts." http://www.purgatory.net/kornelia/1603/red_hair_facts.htm. Retrieved January 27, 2014.

"The Secret of the Tunnels." http://www.shanghaitunnels.info. Retrieved March 10, 2013.

"Siletz Bay Ghost Ship: An Oregon Coast Ghost Story." *Our Oregon Coast*. http://ouroregoncoast.com/lincoln-city-area-guide/1409-siletz-bay-ghost-ship-an-oregon-coast-ghost-story.html. Retrieved October 5, 2013.

"Siletz Bay Lodge." *NWCoast.com*. http://www.nwcoast.com/profile/?city = lincolncity&id = 240. Retrieved October 25, 2013.

State Report Index for OR. *National UFO Reporting Center*. http://www
.nuforc.org/webreports/ndxlOR.html. Retrieved September 2, 2013.

Switzer, Shannon. "Ghost-Dodging in Portland." *National Geographic: Curi-
ous Traveler*, June 27, 2012. http://intelligenttravel.nationalgeographic
.com/2012/06/27/ghost-dodging-in-portland. Retrieved January 27,
2014.

"The Top 5 Most Haunted Spots in Oregon." *Yahoo Voices*, Jan. 19, 2009.
http://voices.yahoo.com/the-top-5-most-haunted-spots-oregon
-2494151.html. Retrieved March 18, 2013.

"Top 10 Waterfalls: View the West's most memorable cascades, from Hawaii
to Yellowstone." *Sunset* magazine. http://www.sunset.com/travel/
outdoor-adventure/top-10-waterfalls-00400000011551. Retrieved November 22, 2013.

"Two of Bend's Most Gruesome Unsolved Crimes: Beware crazies in the
wilderness." *The Source Weekly*, October 24, 2012. http://www
.bendsource.com/bend/two-of-bends-most-gruesome-unsolved-crimes
-beware-crazies-in-the-wilderness/Content?oid = 2186106.   Retrieved
March 29, 2013.

"Understanding the Different Types of Ghosts." *OurCuriousWorld.com*.
http://www.ourcuriousworld.com/TypesofGhosts.htm#p4. Retrieved
September 7, 2013.

"Wallowa   Lake   Monster." *UnknownExplorers.com*.   http://www
.unknownexplorers.com/wallowalakemonster.php. Retrieved November
2, 2013.

"Werewolf sightings/encounters" forum. *Unexplained-Mysteries.com*.
http://www.unexplained-mysteries.com/forum/index.php
?showtopic = 34855&st = 60. Retrieved October 31, 2013.

"What Causes Hostile Hauntings?" *Pinellas Pasco Paranormal/Hostile
Haunts   Specialists.*   http://www.pinellaspascoparanormal.com/
whatcausesbadhaunts.htm. Retrieved October 31, 2013.

"What *is* a Bigfoot, or Sasquatch?" *Bigfoot Field Researchers Organization.*
http://www.bfro.net/gdb/show_FAQ.asp?id = 584. Retrieved September
7, 2013.

Williams, Yona. "Haunted Schools in Oregon." *Unexplainable.net*,
May 4, 2008. http://www.unexplainable.net/ghost-paranormal/haunted
_schools_in_oregon.php. Retrieved September 14, 2013.

"The Witch's Castle—Portland, Oregon." *Northwestern Ghosts and Hauntings*. http://northwesternghostsandhauntings.blogspot.com/2010/11/
witchs-castle-portland-oregon.html. Retrieved August 31, 2013.

"World Famous Jantzen Beach Park." *PdxHistory.com*. http://www
.pdxhistory.com/html/jantzen_beach.html. Retrieved September 8, 2013.

Ziegler, Nathan. "Freaky find in the Cemetery Last Night." http://
www.youtube.com/watch?v = ti4_KA7IjTA. Retrieved January 27, 2014.

Acknowledgments

WRITING A BOOK IS A PROCESS THAT INVOLVES MANY DAYS AND NIGHTS (which stretch into very long and sleepless nights when you already work full time as a professional journalist) and the support of many individuals. Any weakness in this book is mine, but for its strengths there are several people I wish to thank.

Many thanks to Kyle R. Weaver, my editor, who invited me to write this book, my third under his friendly professionalism. He is a gentleman editor of the first class, and my life is richer for being associated with him. His assistant, Brittany Stoner, helped make this a better book with her keen eye and enthusiasm; and illustrator Marc Radle always increases the value of my books with his artwork. (If you don't like what I've written, keep the book anyway just for the illustrations!) Thank you, all and others at Stackpole Books, a quality publisher, who always do such a nice job designing and marketing the product. I'm happy to be a part of the Stackpole family of authors.

I cannot thank enough my small fan club: my eternal sweetheart, Heidi; our son and my best buddy, Brayden; and my mom, Vivian. They encourage and motivate me with their words of wisdom and loving examples. I said it before—Heidi fell in love with a dreamer. I'm glad that dreamer was me. This book is for you, babe!

I appreciate those who've answered questions or shared their stories with me, namely Marie Cuff, executive director of the International Paranormal Reporting Group; Mike Eadie, owner of Hoodoo Antiques in Portland; Anne Hall, executive director of the Lincoln City Historical Museum; and native Oregonian Evee Vann.

I deeply appreciate the friends I've made at Barnes and Noble bookstores in Idaho and Utah for their help in promoting my books and inviting me to signings and other events, and those who've read my books at home, in the classroom, or next to a campfire. It is always nice to hear from you. I hope you like this book.

And, as always, I appreciate the authors and journalists whose books, articles, and websites helped me in the research and writing of this book. As a fellow journalist, I know how thankless that work can be at times. Thank you for your contributions.

About the Author

ANDY WEEKS IS AN AWARD-WINNING JOURNALIST AND THE AUTHOR OF three previous books on history and the paranormal: *Haunted Utah*, *Haunted Idaho*, and *Ghosts of Idaho's Magic Valley*. He has been published in the magazines *Fangoria*, *Northwest Travel*, and *Wild West*, as well as other publications in the United States and United Kingdom.

Other Titles in the

Haunted Series

Haunted Arizona
by Charles A. Stansfield Jr.
978-0-8117-3620-6
Haunted Colorado
by Charles A. Stansfield Jr.
978-0-8117-0855-5
Haunted Connecticut
by Cheri Revai • 978-0-8117-3296-3
Haunted Delaware
by Patricia A. Martinelli
978-0-8117-3297-0
Haunted Florida
by Cynthia Thuma and Catherine Lower
978-0-8117-3498-1
Haunted Georgia
by Alan Brown • 978-0-8117-3443-1
Haunted Hudson Valley
by Cheri Farnsworth
978-0-8117-3621-3
Haunted Idaho
by Andy Weeks • 978-0-8117-1176-0
Haunted Illinois
by Troy Taylor • 978-0-8117-3499-8
Haunted Indiana
by James A. Willis • 978-0-8117-0779-4
Haunted Jersey Shore
by Charles A. Stansfield Jr.
978-0-8117-3267-3
Haunted Kentucky
by Alan Brown • 978-0-8117-3584-1
Haunted Maine
by Charles A. Stansfield Jr.
978-0-8117-3373-1
Haunted Maryland
by Ed Okonowicz • 978-0-8117-3409-7
Haunted Massachusetts
by Cheri Revai • 978-0-8117-3221-5
Haunted Minnesota
by Charles A. Stansfield Jr.
978-0-8117-0014-6
Haunted Missouri
by Troy Taylor • 978-0-8117-1014-5

Haunted New Jersey
by Charles A. Stansfield Jr.
and Patricia A. Martinelli
978-0-8117-3156-0
Haunted New York
by Cheri Revai • 978-0-8117-3249-9
Haunted New York City
by Cheri Revai • 978-0-8117-3471-4
Haunted North Carolina
by Patty A. Wilson • 978-0-8117-3585-8
Haunted Northern California
by Charles A. Stansfield Jr.
978-0-8117-3586-5
Haunted Ohio
by Charles A. Stansfield Jr.
978-0-8117-3472-1
Haunted Pennsylvania
by Mark Nesbitt and Patty A. Wilson
978-0-8117-3298-7
Haunted South Carolina
by Alan Brown • 978-0-8117-3635-0
Haunted Southern California
by Charles A. Stansfield Jr.
978-0-8117-3539-1
Haunted Tennessee
by Alan Brown • 978-0-8117-3540-7
Haunted Texas
by Alan Brown • 978-0-8117-3500-1
Haunted Utah
by Andy Weeks • 978-0-8117-0052-8
Haunted Vermont
by Charles A. Stansfield Jr.
978-0-8117-3399-1
Haunted Virginia
by L. B. Taylor Jr. • 978-0-8117-3541-4
Haunted Washington
by Charles A. Stansfield Jr.
978-0-8117-0683-4
Haunted West Virginia
by Patty A. Wilson • 978-0-8117-3400-4
Haunted Western Pennsylvania
by Patty A. Wilson • 978-0-8117-1197-5
Haunted Wisconsin
by Linda S. Godfrey • 978-0-8117-3636-7

WWW.STACKPOLEBOOKS.COM • 1-800-732-3669